Your Purpose Depends On It

Your Purpose Depends On It

By: Toshia Jordan

XULON PRESS ELITE

Xulon Press Elite
2301 Lucien Way #415
Maitland, FL 32751
407.339.4217
www.xulonpress.com

ISBN-13: 978-1-6628-1891-2
Ebook ISBN-13: 978-1-6628-1892-9

Dedication

To Jamie, my husband, thank you for your continued support and love. We are a great team, and I appreciate all you do for our family. To Langston and Olivia, I am so grateful God choose me to be your mother. You both are growing into amazing individuals, and I couldn't be prouder. I love my family dearly, and I feel blessed that I get to do life with each one of you.

Love You Always

Contents

About the Book

We live in a fallen world, and because of this, bad things happen; fathers leave, people abuse, jobs end, and I could go on. Although we cannot always control what happens, we can control how we respond. We can either choose God's way of handling the situation or the world's way. Often, we choose the world's way due to either lack of knowledge, or it just seems easier. However, choosing the world's way will never end well. We live our lives bound by the strongholds that are created. This most always prevents us from living abundant lives promised to us and distracts us from fulfilling the very purpose of our lives.

Additionally, these attacks on our spirit over time can manifest physically in disease. God says He gives us a choice, life or death, choose life. Choosing life means when unpleasant things happen, we push into God like never before. We allow His Love, Presence, Word, and Spirit to heal us, revealing our new creation. And the wounds that could have been fatal become a catalyst for protecting and saving others. Choose life, for it's the path that leads to wholeness.

Journey with me as I learn to choose life in the seasons of becoming a wife, mother, understanding my identity, and carrying out my purpose. The challenges and joys of life all began to make sense once I learned to surrender. It was only when I learned to surrender and press into God that I began to walk into God's purpose for me. I am still learning to love the journey, not just the destination. There is so much to be gained from the journey. As you read this, I hope that you can gain inspiration for your journey as we travel through the seasons of my life. It is essential for you to learn to embrace the surrender because your purpose depends on it. And your story, like mine, will become a testimony that encourages others to overcome and walk into their purpose.

Think of this book as getting together with your friends. Whenever you are together, your conversation flows to several different topics, and at the end, you leave refreshed and encouraged until the next time. **Your Purpose Depends on It** is that conversation with friends in book form. I hope that when you are finished reading this book, and we have talked about the many aspects of life, including marriage, finances, motherhood, identity, wellness, and our faith, you will leave feeling refreshed and encouraged. So, grab some tea and have a seat at my table. I am so glad you are here.

Pebbles on the Path

Like with a journey we take on foot, we often pick up pebbles that catch our eye. As you journey through this book and life, I encourage you to pick up the pebbles from your path and write them down. Your pebbles may take the form of scripture, a thought, or past memory that jumps out at you. Not everyone likes to journal, but it easy to jot down some significant life experiences and inspiration. Also, make sure to write the date down as well. You will be surprised at what God can show you in this simple exercise. It is also beneficial to see your progress.

Additionally, collecting these pebbles on the path of your life journey will equip you to share key points of your life that may encourage and inspire others. Look for places throughout the book to store your pebbles. You will also find scripture for each journey we take together grouped by theme. Read through the related scripture and highlight the scriptures that speak to you. These scriptures will be a great starting point when you begin to put together a plan that includes believing and confessing God's Word over every area of your life. Now let's go and take a journey of a lifetime, for **Your Purpose Depends on It**!

Something Was Missing

I feel like I have known God forever. I come from a Christian home far from perfect, but we knew how to turn back to God for help and strength. As a child, Sundays consisted of Sunday school, service, and Paw Paw & Maw Maw's House. There we ate and had more church either from my uncles blasting gospel music, a discussion on God being so good, or spontaneous gospel singing sessions. My uncles played instruments that were usually nearby. We had a strong Christian family, but **something was missing**.

Later on, we changed churches, and I gained a core spiritual foundation. I started to learn about God outside of Bible stories and desired to discover more. Even in high school, I would read my Bible often and try to learn the ways of God. This foundation kept me through college. I wasn't perfect, but it kept me, but **something was missing**.

You see, I was a Christian, I went to church, I was a good person, I tried to do good things, but **something was missing**. I wasn't free, and oh how I longed to be free. I identified with a poem written by Stevie Smith entitled "Not Waving but Drowning" for most of my life. I felt like I was waving for help, but all people could see was my performance, and oh how I performed. I rehearsed the lines to every part I played, and I performed. Most of the time, I got standing ovations, but there were times that feedback was less than stellar, and it was draining. And then it happened everything that I had built up for a flawless performance fell away. I quit my job to be a stay-at-home mother. The job was gone, the extra cash was gone, my son didn't care that I had degrees from The University of Chapel Hill and a Master's Degree from UNCC. I had gained weight, and no longer could I fit into my cute clothes. Although my closet was full of high heels from Cole Haan, I couldn't bear walking in them while carrying my new baby boy and all the stuff that came with him. Marriage was hard, and the strain of one income made it harder. I was a Christian, and although The Scripture said that I was an overcomer and the head and not the tail, it sure didn't feel that way. **Something was missing**.

The Two Became One and Multiplied

My husband and I met on my 21st birthday on Franklin St., a popular street near my University. Our courtship was enjoyable for the most part; we had our differences, but we enjoyed each other's company and focused on that. We fell in love by spending our Sundays in the gardens just enjoying being together. He was a photographer, so I become one of his main subjects, and it was good. He helped me think outside the box and do things I didn't normally do. I guess that is all it took because six years later, we married. It was amazing how our family and friends came together to help us with our beautiful wedding. Everyone pitched in. My grandmother's best friend cut absolutely every beautiful hydrangea from her well-groomed bushes for our big day. Friends and family gave money, gifts, and services. It was amazing. Our big day felt blessed and right. And then the process of two becoming one began.

At first, before the children, it was manageable. We usually could work out our differences and make both parties at least ok with the outcome. It helped that we were on the same page on some things like our finances. And when we were on the same page, we worked great as a team. We were paying off debt, enjoying new experiences together, saving for vacations, and later saving for our first home. However, some challenges that we didn't see coming were just around the corner, and we were working with less than a full toolbox. You see, neither of us had fathers living in the home, and examples of good marriages to follow were few and far between. We were in the marriage now, and we were committed to making it work, so I guess we would have to learn along the way. We continued, and we planned for our first trip to Europe. We were excited it was going to be an adventure that we took together. It was all new to us. We had to figure out many things, but we would do it together, and it would be fun. A couple of weeks before we were to leave, I noticed I was super tired. I would come home from work and just sleep. I told my husband if this continues, I am going to need to get checked out. Then it hit me. Could it be? Could I be PREGNANT? Either my husband had been doing some research or just knew because the day I took the test that revealed the beginning of our new life, he walked in the door with sparkling grape juice to celebrate. We were pregnant and on our way to Europe. Let the adventures begin!

Europe was great! Some of the highlights included when we first got there, we picked the wrong transportation and ended up lugging our bags through the streets of France outside of Paris, where the language barrier was more significant. You must also remember that I am newly pregnant. I needed protein, and I needed it now! Oh yeah, and we don't eat pork. So, we were always on the lookout for the nearest cheeseburger. Both Paris and Rome were great! We enjoyed delicious food, incredible sights, and memorable experiences. It was so great for our marriage to take on the unknown and succeed! However, a new adventure awaited us in about nine months. Oh, what an adventure it would be.

Marriage, however, is its own adventure. It is work becoming one. When you add one income to the work of marriage, it becomes incredibly stressful. All the things we used to enjoy had to be downsized. The slabs of salmon, the trips, the nice clothes, the fun date nights all had no place in our current life or budget, and that was hard. We knew it was the right thing for our children, but it didn't make it any easier. When you put them side-by-side, I didn't care about a fancy dress, a new car, and a bigger house. We were choosing to train up our children ourselves, which I felt was what God wanted us to do and was very important. But when our finances became strained, we began to question was this the right thing to do? I felt like we were in too deep, and yet again, I was not waving but drowning. You see, I watched my mother struggle and strive with finances, and I was determined not to be in that place. So, I went to college and worked hard to paid bills, even if that meant going without food. I paid my bills first. My thinking was to keep everything current and on time, and I could stay far away from that place I knew so often. The place of wondering how a bill was going to get paid, praying that the lights didn't get cut off and that we had water when we needed it. I was done with that place. I never wanted to go back, but here I was, facing what I tried so hard to avoid. Although it was hard, we continued to believe. We believed that God had a plan to prosper us and not to harm us. And that God was going to do a miraculous work that no eye had seen, no ear had heard, and no mind had imagined because we loved Him. Because we did the thing, He asked of us and focused on training up our children; He would keep His promise to us and provide for us according to His riches in glory. During this season, God promised, *if you keep your eyes on me, you will walk on water*. God's promise assured me that I would walk on the same water that I felt like I was drowning in for so many years. Through experience, God began to show me that I didn't need to be rescued by people, I just needed to focus on Him, and He would cause me to rise above. He is amazing because He was with us every step of the way.

He provided for us. He made a way out of no way many times. I would have desires I didn't even share with others, and they would come to pass. He even kept reassuring us that this was his plan for our children and our family. This season was extremely hard. I wanted to give up at times. However, God would give me the strength to keep moving forward. I kept believing the promise that if I kept seeking the Kingdom first, God would take care of my marriage, my children, my finances, and me. He would take care of it all. I now know that being in that place was a setup for deliverance, but then I felt like I was drowning with all the new responsibilities and worries. I lost my sense of false control with marriage and children, and my false stability was shaking, but that is just what I needed. We had no real answers and no road map except for His promises. All we knew is we wanted something different for our children. We were committed to figuring out what that was. Now looking back at it, it was astonishing how we were in the furnace, but we didn't smell like smoke. Only God can do that! I think what sustained us was God's grace and the fact we were committed no matter what. We loved God, so it had to get better, right?

It did, but not immediately. We had to walk through it. God is amazing, and He blesses the way He wants to bless. Repeatedly, over and over, He has shown us that what may seem like our reality is not His. Our job is to trust in Him and Him alone. With the financial strain, you have to know that season of marriage was no walk in the park. Remember, we were working with less than a full toolbox. We made many of the typical mistakes like blaming each other, not properly communicating, hurtful words, distance, misplaced expectations, etc. Many times, I wanted to give up, but that wasn't a real option. I had made this marriage covenant before my Lord and given my everything to ensure our kids would have a solid foundation. I couldn't bear the responsibility of any negative effects on my kids coming from a broken home. However, I knew what we were modeling wasn't ideal either. So, I continued to trust God. He had promised if I focus on Him, He would take care of everything concerning me. When I turned to Him, He gave me strength, and I was able to keep moving forward. I would pray crafted prayers, which were very helpful, especially when I was so frustrated, and I didn't have the right words to say. I also realized from my past brokenness that I was not letting my husband lead our family. Honestly, I didn't trust him to lead. I had come from a home where Mom had to take care of everything regardless if there was a male present or not. I never had a male step into his rightful place and take care of me, so sometimes it was even hard for me to trust God. As you can imagine, If I was having trouble trusting God, how in the world could I trust a mere mortal. However, I knew it was time to trust God and do it His way concerning our home, although it was painful. God has a specific order for a reason, and we were out of order. I needed to be in alignment with my Heavenly Father, so there was one thing to do, hand over the reins. I ask my husband to forgive me and began to slowly release the tight grip I had on trying to secure our family. It's funny when I write this out because although I thought I was controlling something the whole time, I wasn't, and God just waited patiently for me to get that and just let go. I had to trust Him to take care of me, not my husband. Now, I have to admit that I am not perfect, and at times I do try to grab the reigns again, but God is still working on me.

At times, I would get mad at my husband because some of his decisions didn't make me feel safe and secure. This strained our relationship because I was looking at my husband to meet that need, which is not wrong, but ultimately it first needed to be met by God. He promises that He will never leave us or forsake us, and through the past years, I have the experience to back that up. It isn't easy, but what began to help me was focusing on my purpose and diving into the Word of God to console me. I would sometimes go to bed listening to The Word. God's word during this time was truly life-giving. In addition, support and encouragement from family and friends and solid biblical teachings helped me through this long, difficult season in which I learned that God is my source, not my husband. God also spoke over me through a customer that because I had been faithful, my whole house would be saved. I continued to stand on God's promises. I brought back my scripture for the journey to remind me to get serious about meditating and confessing the word over my marriage. I also followed some of the practical steps below, and in time God started to heal our marriage (**See Thinkable Thoughts for Marriage**). I would love to say that our marriage is perfect now, but we are still ironing out the kinks. However, I am confident that we will get it with God's help, and He will restore and make our union new because we trust in Him.

Make a Choice

Love is funny. I use to wrestle with the fact that if my husband did the "right" thing, it would make it easy, and everything would be great. I am a loving person and fairly easy to get along with, I thought, but we would butt heads. We would argue, and I would plead my case over and over for him just to change. Shouldn't he go first? He is the head of the household and is supposed to be leading. Shouldn't he go first? However, one day while listening to a Christian meditation on love, I realized that I loved people who were easy to love and loved me back. If you showed any, and I mean any signs of being "special," I separated myself quickly. Unfortunately or fortunately, that isn't the love Jesus modeled. I had to love even when it was hard. I had to choose to love and choose not to be offended. These were hard choices to make. It is much easier when you don't live with the person, so up close and personal, but the marriage relationship is up close and personal. And just like everything that God requires of us, He will enable you to do it if you submit to His way. I have to continue to submit to His ways, although some days are better than others.

I had to recommit to the work involved in making our marriage better. Our marriage was struggling, but too much was at stake. I believe marriage is one of the foundational earthly relationships that affect our outlook on many things. Our relationship with our earthly father is another one of those relationships. These are foundational relationships because the relationship with your earthly father affects how you see our Heavenly Father. The marriage relationship is an example of Christ and the Church. We must work to mend these relationships if at all possible. In addition, my babies needed the stability of a home with two loving parents. It was time to get over myself and submit to God's way. It was time to choose differently.

When I think about the way God loves me, I think about His love being unconditional and sacrificial. I am so glad God doesn't love me based on my behavior and performance. And I needed to stop loving my husband based on his behavior. I just needed to love, for the Bible says that love covers a multitude of sins. God also loves sacrificially, and for me, it meant there is too much at stake to continue to insist that I have it my way. Yes, it would have been so much easier and delightful if my husband would just have assumed the position of love first. However, if that would have happened, I would not have had the opportunity to learn to love based on Jesus's model. I had to sacrifice my way for God's way and allow His strength to help me in choosing love even when it was less than desirable. I had to choose not to be offended when many times, it would be the natural response. My older sister shed some light on offense that spoke to me. She said that offense stops the flow of the Holy Spirit, which prevents communication and stunts growth. And I feel both me and my husband had let offense prevent us from proper communication. I would say, please hand me that green pen, but he would hear I am going to break that green pen. It was amazing how there was a real block to our communication. I feel like the offenses we had collected over the years had opened a door for satan and blocked the Holy Spirit's flow in our relationship. And we are not having that! The same Christian meditation mentioned above also mentions focusing on "lesser things," causing you not to show love.

I believe those "lesser things" could be all those daily opportunities of offense. Instead of collecting offenses like stamps or coins, we need to learn the "art of ignoring." Now let me explain. I am not talking about the ignoring that results when there is a communication breakdown. I am talking about not focusing on every single misstep your spouse displays. We are human, and we will not be perfect until Jesus comes back, although we continually strive toward that standard. When we learn the "art of ignoring" some of those missteps and "lesser things" aren't as important as peace in the house. Regularly practicing this would put us in a place where we could walk in the unity and oneness necessary for a husband and wife, allowing us to become all God created us to be together.

Above all, love each other deeply, because love covers over a multitude of sins. 1 Peter 4:8 (NIV)

No Longer the Dating Game, Its now the Waiting Game

I believe a key to a successful marriage is the woman's ability to stand strong while her husband finds his way and walks in it. This is just my opinion, but many times I feel motherhood and the sacrifices that come with that start women on the journey a little earlier than men on average. The waiting game is difficult. However, like I keep mentioning, there is too much at stake to give in to the alternatives. The woman has to seek God with all her heart to endure. Giving up is not an option, which feels extremely overwhelming. You feel trapped, and that never feels good. However, the alternative undermines the stability that two loving parents in the same household give. God's design is perfect, and while He can and will restore, we can prevent a lot of hardship by tapping into the Holy Spirit on the inside of us. Besides, divorce opens up a new can of worms. I think the Fireproof movie describes it best when it uses the example of a salt and pepper shaker been superglued together. The shakers cannot be separated unless damage is done. Another good reason to endure is that marriage represents Christ and the Church to the world, and for this and other reasons, there is an intense attack on the marriage relationship.

We also can't stay and resort to bitterness. Bitterness makes you physically sick and miserable and leads to depression. It seems not fair. Right? Not only do you have to stay in an unhappy marriage, but you have to have a good attitude about it. However, if we submit to God's way (there is that word again)😊, He will give us tools not only to go through but grow through.

I like to call these tools "assists" (like in basketball). We need to provide our husbands "assist" to drive to the goal, hopefully fast, with the goal being a strong, healthy marriage. Some of these assists include praying for your husband. At times this is very hard, and that is why I love using crafted prayers. At first, you may not feel like it but commit (a choice) to read a marriage-related prayer daily until you have your own words to pray. Secondly, you have to show love despite your husband's actions or inactions. This is when we practice moving in the opposite spirit and use those Fruits of The Spirits. Remember, it is all about choice. Although sometimes this can be extremely hard, when you submit to God's ways, especially when it is difficult, you gain ground quicker. Thirdly, this assist I like to title "call a brother up." Usually, when talking about accountability, you will always hear individuals say give them a call to keep them accountable. However, this "call a brother up" is to confess who they are in Christ before you see it. I think we have a responsibility as wives to "call a brother up" into his proper place. By doing this, you are essentially calling them up into their rightful place and confessing God's Word over them.

For me, the most significant turning point for our marriage was when a lie was revealed. I was in a rough place. I felt trapped and hopeless. Most of the time, I would just go through motions, almost numb to my true feelings. When I would allow the least amount of feeling to rise to the surface, they would engulf me like an ocean wave. I felt like I was gasping for air under an insurmountable, suffocating wave. I knew I had to stay in the marriage, I knew I didn't need to be bitter, but I couldn't make the sadness go away. After desiring a great marriage, I couldn't believe that it was in such a difficult place. The measures I had put into place to make sure I was always financially secure, which was extremely important to me, had eroded. At the lowest times of my life, like the financial difficulties, the person I had chosen to weather life's storms was at odds with me. I morphed into a tense ball of pain, and it wasn't cute. I knew my husband loved me, but this season was long and difficult, and we were both tired. Then one day, during quarantine, it happened. I had listened to a speaker during a zoom meeting, and she shared **Exodus 14:13-14**.

The New Living Version (NIV) reads.

> Moses answered the people, "Do not be afraid. Stand firm and you will see the deliverance the Lord will bring you today. The Egyptians you see today you will never see again. The Lord will fight for you; you need only to be still." Then the Lord said to Moses, "Why are you crying out to me? Tell the Israelites to move on. Raise your staff and stretch out your hand over the sea to divide the water so that the Israelites can go through the sea on dry ground. **Exodus 14:13-16 (NIV)**

I like the New Living Translation as well. It reads.

> But Moses told the people, "Don't be afraid.
> Just stand still and watch the Lord rescue
> you today. The Egyptians you see today will
> never be seen again. The Lord Himself will
> fight for you. Just stay calm. Then the Lord
> said to Moses, "Why are you crying out to
> me? Tell the people to get moving! Pick
> up your staff and raise your hand over the
> sea. Divide the water so the Israelites can
> walk through the middle of the sea on dry
> ground. **Exodus 14:13-16 (NLT)**

I was inspired by the message, thinking that it solely spoke to me about trusting God related to my purpose and this season of uncertainty pertaining to COVID-19. It was a great message, and I felt inspired. I needed to be productive that weekend, so I began to sort through some papers and found a "letter" that Mom had sent to me in May 2004. At this time, mom didn't have an email account. She would send us letters, and at the top, it would read Mom's email. I just love my Mom! Here is the letter or Mom's email😊 I found.

Mom's E-mail

May 2004

Hi Toshia,

Hope you are having a great day, and a great week. Sending you a few lines from the Word of God.

Exodus 15:2-3(KJV)

The Lord is my strength and song, and He is become my salvation! He is my God, and I will prepare Him a habitation; My Father's God and I will exalt Him. The Lord is a man of war! The Lord is His name.

Exodus 14:13-14

And Moses said unto the people, fear ye not, stand still, and see the salvation of the Lord, Which He will show to you today; for the Egyptians whom ye have seen today, ye shall see them again no more forever. The Lord will fight for you, and ye shall hold your peace.

Psalm 48:14

For this God is our God forever and ever; He will be our guide even unto death.

II Samuel 22:33

God is my strength and power, and He maketh my way perfect.

Psalm 118:14

The Lord is my strength and song and is become my salvation.

Philippians 4:13

I can do all things through Christ which strengtheneth me.

I Love You!
Mom

Special note before I continue ...

This Letter (Mom's E-mail) demonstrates the power of the Word of God. It does not return void; it is alive and did a work in my life 16 years after she had written it down.

The love and legacy of a mother who was determined to sow the seed of faith and God's love made a difference.

There it was again Exodus 14:13-14! I marveled at the fact that it appeared twice, and then I went to another section of papers I needed to sort and found these words written on a random sheet of paper

"Stand still and let God fight Your battle. He will be your strength."

I can't speak for anyone else, but many times when God has been trying to get my attention, He has used repetition or a lot of something like spider webs you will hear about later. I was drawn to spend some time with Him, and I am so glad I did! He began to reveal that I felt so hopeless and sad about our marriage because I believed a lie. I believed that I was stuck in a marriage that couldn't be repaired. All I could see was years passing, and our marriage still stuck in struggle. But God had been making Himself known to me as a Way Maker, especially in our finances, and He was on the verge of showing me that same nature in our marriage. I will try to capture all the life-changing truth that He revealed through Exodus 14:13-16.

His plan of Deliverance for Our Marriage based on Exodus 14:13-14

1. Do Not Be Afraid, Do Not Fear

Our God is a Warrior and Waymaker known to make a way out of no way. Believe it! Just because you can't figure out a plan that works doesn't mean this is how the story ends. Our God is a master at miracles. We don't have to be afraid. There is no need to lose hope and despair because of the current marriage challenges. Our Father has a plan, and His plans don't fail.

2. Stand Firm and Watch for Deliverance

Psalm 27:13-14 sums up points 1 and 2 in this way, "I would have despaired unless I had believed that I would see the goodness of the Lord In the land of the living. Wait for the Lord; Be strong and let your heart take courage; Yes, wait for the Lord." Stand on God's Word and His Character. You must believe in His ability and desire to deliver you enough that you watch for the deliverance. You anticipate the victory. It makes a difference.

3. The Lord Will Fight for You

This is a fight you can't fight on your own. I know for me, I tried to say the right thing that would bring enlightenment, but it was always construed into something else. No plan I made would work. I had to surrender and trust God to do the fighting for me. It is just like when Moses held up his hands (like in a surrendered position), they were winning the fight. I had to surrender and let go of what I thought would make the marriage work better.

4. Stay Calm (Be still) – Quietness (rest) and Confidence (trust)

When I looked at the state of our marriage and the years passing, I tended to want to jump into action. I tried to save the sinking ship, but I needed to resist that and rest in God. That rest not only shows that you have confidence in Him to make the difference, but it also continues to build your trust in His ability and His desire to do it for you. Repent that you thought your way was the way and submit to God and His way. Rest by spending time with Him.

> This is what the Sovereign Lord, the Holy One of Israel says: "Only in returning to me and resting in me will you be saved. In quietness and confidence is your strength. But you will have none of it. **Isaiah 30:15**

5. Move Forward – When you take that first step (raising the rod and moving toward the water), you must move forward in love, responding in

faith, as though God has already done the work. When you do the little, God will do the big. He will part the sea to reveal dry land. He will make a way that wasn't there before you took a step of faith.

6. He Will Guide You and Show You Where to Go

You may ask, how do I move forward? He will guide you and show you. It may seem awkward at first to hold your husband's hand or lay your head on his lap, but God will lead you, and as you are obedient to His leading, the walls will fall, the sea will open, and victory for your marriage will become imminent.

I will instruct you and teach you in the way you should go; I will guide you with My eye. **Psalm 32:8 (NKJV)**

I felt like the Lord was saying to me.

If you believe that it is so and that I will fight for you related to your marriage, you can move forward as if it is already done. You don't have to despair and lose hope. You don't have to stay clenched and tense without peace. You don't have to eat for comfort because you feel stuck. You are free, says the Lord, victory is sure, move

> **forward, walk in love, stay calm, trust me,
> and watch me fight for you!**

Praise the Lord!!!! The walls are falling! The lie has been revealed! I am not stuck! My Father is a Way Maker! Marriage is hard. Two are becoming one, and that doesn't feel good. However, God is faithful, and He promises to be with us every step of the way. God's strength is made known to us in the times we are weak. When we want to say we are done because this is ridiculous, but we submit to His way of doing things anyway. God's strength is made known to us when He gently says, *no, you are not done, and this is what you are going to do*, and you listen. It's then that His peace engulfs you, eases your heart, and lessens the burden, enabling you to keep walking out His purpose for your marriage. If we do it God's way, no matter how we feel, I am confident that the gift of marriage will be revealed.

God not only showed Himself faithful as it related to our marriage. He also did it as it related to our finances. Before working part-time at a Christian bookstore, I had been a stay-at-home Mom for over ten years. When the Christian bookstore closed, I was in between working on what I felt was a venture of purpose and considering a local 10-week entrepreneur class. In the meantime, God opened a door for me to work remotely full-time. I was hesitant because I didn't know how I would juggle every-thing, and there was travel involved. However, I continued forward. It almost felt like I was gently pushed from behind, although reluctant to move forward. I thank God for the gentle push because a month and a half after I started to work, quarantine happened. Because of quarantine, I was able to work full-time from home while my kids were in the virtual academy, and the travel that concerned me turned to virtual meetings. God is amazing! I felt like at the beginning of quarantine, it would be a time of opportunity and repositioning, but I didn't know it would happen as it did. Within months things that we had waited years to accomplish were completed. I still stand amazed at how He worked on our behalf and how He loves and guides me. There was a lot of uncertainty, and a lot of things were going on. However, even in all of that, God can still bless, and He did that for us. There is still a lot that needs to happen. I don't know all the answers, but I do know that God is faithful. He will finish what He starts.

Thinkable Thoughts for Marriage

- **Pray for Your Husband & Marriage Daily**

- **Don't be easily offended (Learn the Art of Ignoring ;)**

- **Remember you are on the same team**

- **See your spouse as God sees them**

- **Think on these things (don't rehearse all the wrong capture your thoughts)**

- **Let God love your spouse through you**

- **Becoming friends again**

- **Forgive because God said so and forgive quickly**

- **Don't go to bed angry if you can help it**

- **Call up (build-up don't tear down)**

- **Believe that God can make all things new**

- **Remember that neither of you are perfect**

- **Seek first the Kingdom of God, and everything will be added that includes a great marriage**

- **Forget those things in the past and press toward the future**

- **Reset and Reset again – nothing to lose, but everything to gain**

Scripture for the Journey: Marriage

Two are better than one because they have a good return for their labor. For if either of them falls, the one will lift up his companion. But woe to the one who falls when there is not another to lift him up. Furthermore, if two lie down together they keep warm, but how can one be warm alone? And if one can overpower him who is alone, two can resist him. **A cord of three strands is not quickly torn apart. Ecclesiastes 4:9-12 (NIV)**

Let all bitterness and wrath and anger and clamor and slander be put away from you, along with all malice. Be kind to one another, tenderhearted, forgiving one another, as God in Christ forgave you. **Ephesians 4:31-32 (ESV)**

Above all, love each other deeply, because love covers over a multitude of sins. **1 Peter 4:8 (NIV)**

Dear friends, since God loved us that much, we surely ought to love each other. No one has ever seen God. But if we love each other,

God lives in us, and his love is brought to full expression in us. **1 John 4:11-12 (NLT)**

And I will ask the Father and He will give you another Advocate (Comforter, Encourager, or Counselor) who will never leave you. He is the Holy Spirit who leads into all truth. The world cannot receive him, because it isn't looking for him and doesn't recognize him. But you know him because he lives with you now and later will be in you. **John 14:16-17 (NLT)**

Moses answered the people, "Do not be afraid. Stand firm and you will see the deliverance the Lord will bring you today. The Egyptians you see today you will never see again. The Lord will fight for you; you need only to be still." **Exodus 14:13-14 (NIV)**

Scripture for the Journey: Finances

"Therefore, do not worry, saying, 'What shall we eat?' or 'What shall we drink?' or 'What shall we wear?' For after all these things the Gentiles seek. For your heavenly Father knows that you need all these things. But seek first the kingdom of God and His righteousness, and all these things shall be added to you. **Matthew 6:31-33(NKJV)**

If you then, being evil, know how to give good gifts to your children, how much more will your Father who is in heaven give what is good to those who ask Him! **Matthew 7:11 (NKJV)**

Give generously to him and do so without a grudging heart; then because of this, the Lord your God will bless you in all your work and in everything you put your hand to. **Deuteronomy 15:10 (NIV)**

Now He who supplies seed to the sower and bread for food will supply and multiply your seed for sowing and increase the harvest of your righteousness. **2 Corinthians 9:10 (ESV)**

And my God shall supply all your need according to His riches in glory by Christ Jesus. **Philippians 4:19 (NKJV)**

The angel of the Lord encamps all around those who fear Him, and delivers them. Oh, taste and see that the Lord is good; Blessed is the man who trusts in Him! Oh, fear the Lord, you His saints! There is no want to those who fear Him. The young lions lack and suffer hunger, but those who seek the Lord shall not lack any good thing. **Psalm 34:7-10 (NKJV)**

Pebbles from the Path: Marriage and Finances

Use this section to write notes from this chapter or jot down things that come to mind from your life in the areas of marriage and finance.

_____

_____

_____

_____

_____

_____

_____

_____

_____

_____

She Shall Be Called Blessed

Although I am sure God had been working on me before I ask Him to, I feel like motherhood set in motion the journey of a lifetime. Don't get me wrong, motherhood is amazing. It is one of the hardest things I have ever done, but I would do it over and over again to get my babies. I think motherhood is definitely part of that sanctification process they talk about because if you want to do it right (and I did), it takes every morsel of your being, and it starts at conception.

Early on, I came across some wonderful books that help me think about pregnancy and labor differently than

I had ever imagined. I began to start confessing Scripture in a way I had never done before. Confessing Scripture was amazing for me during that season of my life, and it set a foundation for other areas as well. I spent a lot of time in those books, reading related Scripture and confessing God's word concerning the matter. It was necessary because I was going on an unfamiliar journey, not only unfamiliar to me but no one that I knew had believed God for a supernatural childbirth in this way. I wanted to believe God for that. I felt like it was possible deep inside, but the books confirmed my feelings. I was confident and ready to believe God for a childbirth that didn't line up with statistics and doctor's facts. A childbirth that glorified God, and I am blessed to say that I had two. Both of my pregnancies were great. I had back pain but no other real consistent issues unless I tried to do too much. If I tried to do too much, all I had to do is slow down, and I would recover. With my first pregnancy, I remember labor starting. I call the doctor. He assured me that it would take a long time before I delivered because it was my first child. He suggested a bath and trying to get some sleep. He said he would see me in the morning. I knew we had a drive ahead of us and felt like we should go on, but my doctor knows. Right? He is the doctor. Of course, he knows. However, after praying, I remember what I had believed for, and it had nothing to do with my doctor's statistics. We decide to go, and just as the doctor is getting in, I am pushing. On the second push, my baby boy was here. My doctor said, "Way to go from 0 to 60." What he didn't know is that I was believing and confessing God for a supernatural birth, which supersedes his natural training.

I remember with my little girl. I got to the hospital, and I felt sure it was close to pushing time. They said I was only 1 to 1 ½ centimeters dilated. They said I should go home and labor some more there. Before I could think, I confidently told them to give me an hour. Again, I had been believing and confessing God's Word with this pregnancy, so it was prayer time. My doula was great because she read my scriptures and confessions over me. After one hour they returned to check me, and to their surprise I was in active labor. In this season, I learned the power of believing and confessing God's Word. God's Word is always a game-changer.

Although pregnancy went well, and God definitely showed up in the labor room, there were some challenges I didn't plan. Unfortunately, on-call the night I went into labor with my daughter was a less than pleasant midwife that I had to endure. And afterward, they would not let my son stay overnight, so my husband and son had to leave each night and go home. In addition, my family couldn't visit because they all had sick children. These issues, paired with the fact my hormones were all over the place, began a time of depression that I would experience on and off in the coming years. However, I learned a valuable lesson during my time in the hospital. God can keep you in your valleys! Although I love it when it works out as planned, I experienced that God can keep me in the valley. This message would prove to be most valuable in the coming years because we would go through multiple financial challenges that would strain our marriage. I experienced firsthand the scripture that reads

> **"Therefore, I am now going to allure her; I will lead her into the wilderness and speak tenderly to her. Hosea 2:14 (NIV)**

I have grown so much after becoming a mother. My husband and I realized that we are just stewards over God's beloved children. We have the amazing job of caring for, loving, and training up these awesome little individuals. It was important for us to do the best job possible, no matter the sacrifice. So, when we felt like God's plan was for me to stay at home with our kids, it was done without hesitation. Somehow, I was able to completely shut off my desire for shopping. I used to love to shop for clothes and shoes. However, to make this work with one income, I disappeared into ill-fitting clothes and worn shoes. It was ok because when my children were small, I didn't go to many places. However, the one difficult place I did go to was church. I couldn't justify not attending because I didn't have the latest outfit, so I would put on my best and hold my head high. Church became extremely hard for me at times because not only did I have to pour myself into clothes that hadn't fit in years, I felt like I had to pretend everything was great. I would push to get to church, dreading every step, and then plead with the ushers to let me sit in the back. It is only by God's grace that I kept going during some of the most difficult seasons. My desire to stay close to my Source and for my kids to be in the church made the difference.

Although I had some difficult times, I was blessed to be home with my babies, and God always provided. When extreme couponing became popular, I was right there with the best of them. It was such a blessing for our family. I remember the excitement of getting so many needed items practically free, but it was stressful for me as well. We would have a certain amount of money for food and household items, so one couponing mistake could be disastrous, I felt. I would pour over my list over and over, calculating and researching. I would be so devasted if I made a mistake. I don't remember the exact time I decide to retire my coupon binder, but I did gain a sense of relief, although it had been a blessing for our family. I also did search engine and customer review programs that give me regular Amazon gift cards. I would save those up to get everything from supplements to home décor. I had over $1000 worth of Amazon gift cards given to me the last time I had counted. God always provided for us! We had one income for around ten years, and we never went without shelter, food, or any necessity. God is just amazing like that. God is faithful!

Other things that I learned while staying at home were the importance of doing my work unto the Lord, flow cleaning, maximizing the times I had energy, the benefit of a home manager, and using essential oils. Constantly, being on and needed gets tiring quickly. For me, I had to remember that I was doing my work unto the Lord even when I was doing the same thing multiple times a day. And at the end of the day, it looked like I had done nothing. Because I thrive on making lists and checking off to-dos, this was very hard for me. However, when you reflect on the fact that you are growing little humans. The fact that God is using you to set some core foundational pieces in place that will make a difference in His Kingdom makes the monotony of it all feel better. This is true no matter what messages you may receive from others who simply don't understand the valuable work you are doing.

I also used flow cleaning and maximizing the times I had energy. Flow cleaning is just cleaning as you go. Not necessarily cleaning as the mess is being made, but in the flow with other activities that you are doing. For example, before jumping in the shower, clean the bathroom, or while you are making dinner, clean the kitchen. I love flow cleaning because it feels less like cleaning, and you can get so much done without all the dread. I also made a home manager. My home manager is a binder that has every-thing I need to manage our home. The home manager includes everything from our budget, cleaning schedules, appliance information, babysitter info, and encouragement for the journey. It was truly rewarding to see my husband using and walking around with our home manager. Proving that our home manager was really useful.

And essential oils, oh how I love thee, let me count the ways! Before getting Young Living essential oils, I had not slept through the night since kids. I didn't know what it was like anymore to lay down at night and not wake up until the next morning. When I started using Young Living lavender and rosemary at night, I started sleeping through the night again, and wow the feeling! Sleep is important for so many functions in your body, and to be able to get great sleep by adding some drops of oil in my diffuser at night, simply priceless. We use oils to support our immune systems, digestive systems, aid in balancing my hormones, and all the "lovely" issues that come with that time of the month, and many more things. If you haven't tried them, you must give quality essential oils a try. It has changed my life and helped me as a mother. I like to call essential oils God's provision because they are! God blessed me to consistently get my essential oils even before working, which was a blessing. We use essential oils daily. They are one of this Mom's first lines of defense. I truly believe that essential oils are a blessing from God, and every time I opened my wooden chest full of these beneficial oils, I felt like God was saying, *I have you, I love you, and I am the Father that gives gifts better than any earthly father.*

Worth

Ten years later, I began to panic because I had lost myself in the role of mother. I didn't know who I was outside of that role, and I was afraid it was too late for many of my dreams to come to pass. However, I kept being reminded that God has me exactly where He wants me, and He would restore the years. This restoration would not be typical, and it would not be drawn out because with Him, what would usually take long periods can happen instantly.

So, my focus became training up my children in the ways of God. And actually, that was a passion of mine for my kids from the very beginning. I remember having a desire to instill biblical principles in my 1-year-old son, Langston. To begin instilling Biblical principles at an early age, I searched for Christian-themed birthday ideas for his 2nd birthday and was unhappy with what I found, so God gave me the "God Made Me" themed birthday idea. I was pleased with the party's results and reactions, so I thought it would be excellent to share the ideas. God instructs us to share His principles with our children. How great it is to share His principles not only at church but in daily activities and special times, like their birthday. Soon after that, God flooded me with numerous birthday themes and Seeds That Last, my ministry was born. Now I have fifteen Christian-themed birthday party packages developed from the desire to instill biblical principles in my children. For me, Seeds that Last was about sowing core Biblical principles into my children earlier than I remember so that they could walk them out in their teens. The ministry's vision is to see all children walking out Biblical principles as a teenager. What a powerful force for the Kingdom of God.

From this, I focused my attention on developing other resources that not only could be used for training up children but encouraging and equipping women, especially mothers and those who desired wellness based on biblical principles. This helped me feel like I had more purpose, but it wasn't bringing in money. And as I said before, one income is hard, very hard. I was feeling the pressure of the role of being a wife, mom, volunteer, and now I needed to figure out how to add employee or entrepreneur. I had so many great ideas, but I couldn't figure out how to make them work. It always seemed that I needed money to make money. In addition, I didn't feel like my husband could understand the challenge of balancing and calculating the kid's well-being in every move I made. The employee option was difficult because my kids attended a year-round school at the time, which meant that they were in school for nine weeks and tracked out for three weeks. To find a job that accommodated 9:30 am to 3 pm, work nine weeks and three weeks off was like looking for a needle in a haystack. However, God gave that needle to me.

During a time of desperation, I started applying for part-time jobs. I started an application for a part-time position at a Christian Bookstore, but before I could finish it, I remembered the kids were tracking out for not three weeks but four weeks this time. I threw up my hands and left the application incomplete. I actually forgot about starting it until one night. I was talking to God as I was getting in bed, and I was once again frustrated with our financial situation. As I was slipping under the covers I passionately said to God, if you want me to have a part-time job, you have to give me one that works with my family's schedule. I don't know why, but I casually picked my phone to check my email. This was weird because I was lying down to sleep. I found an email stating I know it has been a couple of months since you applied, but we wonder if you are still interested in the part-time position at the bookstore. I couldn't believe my eyes! Could this be real? Could God just have answered my prayer instantly? The answer is yes; God answered my prayer and gave me a needle in a haystack. My hours ranged from 9:30am to 3pm during the week and Saturdays. During track out, I worked in the evenings and Saturdays. My husband would meet me and grab the kids when I worked evenings. I enjoyed my job. God is simply amazing.

I will have to say when I first received word that I got the job. I panicked. I hadn't worked outside of our home in 10 years. How would I balance it all? I never worked retail; can I do this? Oh, what about that pay? It was a major pay cut. I even got angry at my husband because he was excited and ready to quit his part-time job, which I had prayed that he would be able to quit. God quickly calmed my fears and refocused me with the words, ***This is not about a job. It is about your PURPOSE!*** And just like that, I was off. It felt good to be working and bringing in some money. I loved helping people find resources for their spiritual journey and just being a smiling face to someone who may need it. And the cherry on the top was that part of my job consisted of praying for others, leading bible studies, and storytime for the kids. Only God can do that! And He did it for me! I can't wait to see what else He has planned for me.

A Mom's Reflections

I wouldn't change staying at home with my children, even with all the challenges we faced. I not only enjoyed watching them grow but all of our wonderful experiences together. They made me brave and pushed me to heights I never imagined because I wanted the best for them. I know we are all partial when it comes to our children, but I am so proud of my babies. They are developing into amazing individuals. They are not perfect, but they have a sincere love for God and others. They are self-motivated and strive for excellence. I truly believe that they are who they are because my husband and I were obedient to God and made the hard decision for me to stay-at-home with them. All the difficulties and struggles fade away compared to the benefits of being home with my babies.

Mom's Tips for Success

- **Spending time with God is the key to your success.**

- **Know that you will not do it in your own strength. Ask the Holy Spirit for help.**

- **Know the time of the day that you are most productive and schedule your day accordingly.**

- **Learn to delegate. Even small children can help.**

- Schedule "Me" time. You will not be good for anyone overworked, broken down, and ill.

- Schedule date nights. The family unit is only as strong as your marriage.

- Choose three main tasks to get done each day if you do more, great!

- Take breaks throughout the day.

- Keep Your Home Manager Notebook updated.

2012 Seeds That Last Home Manager

Scripture for the Journey: Motherhood

Sons are a heritage from the Lord, children a reward from Him. Like arrows in the hands of a warrior are sons born in one's youth. Blessed is the man whose quiver is full of them. They will not be put to shame when they contend with their enemies in the gate. **Psalm 127:3-5 (NIV)**

These commandments that I give you today are to be on your hearts. Impress them on your children. Talk about them when you sit at home and when you walk along the road, when you lie down and when you get up. Tie them as symbols on your hands and bind them on your foreheads. Write them on the doorframes of your houses and on your gates. **Deuteronomy 6:6-9 (NIV)**

Whatever you do, work at it with all your heart, as working for the Lord, not for human masters, since you know that you will receive an inheritance from the Lord as a reward. It is the Lord Christ you are serving. **Colossians 3:23-24 (NIV)**

Train a child in the way he should go and when he is old he will not turn from it. **Proverbs 22:6 (NIV)**

Children, obey your parents in the Lord, for this is right. Honor your father and mother – which is the first commandment with a promise- that it may go well with you and that you may enjoy long life on the earth. **Ephesians 6:1-3 (NIV)**

Rejoice in the Lord always. I will say it again: Rejoice! Let your gentleness be evident to all. The Lord is near. Do not be anxious about anything, but in every situation, by prayer and petition, with thanksgiving, present your requests to God. And the peace of God, which transcends all understanding, will guard your hearts and your minds in Christ Jesus. Finally, brothers and sisters, whatever is true, whatever is noble, whatever is right, whatever is pure, whatever is lovely, whatever is admirable—if anything is excellent or praiseworthy—think about such things. Whatever you have learned or received or heard from me, or seen in me— put it into practice. And the God of peace will be with you. **Philippians 4:4-9 (NIV)**

As Jesus and his disciples were on their way, he came to a village where a woman named Martha opened her home to him. She had a sister called Mary, who sat at the Lord's feet listening to what he said. But Martha was distracted by all the preparations that had to be made. She came to him and asked, "Lord, don't you care that my sister has left me to do the work by myself? Tell her to help me!" "Martha, Martha," the Lord answered, "you are worried and upset about many things, but few things are needed—or indeed only one Mary has chosen what is better, and it will not be taken away from her." **Luke 10: 38-42 (NIV)**

His divine power has given us everything we need for a godly life through our knowledge of Him who called us by His own glory and goodness. **2 Peter 1:3 (NIV)**

"Not by might nor by power, but by My Spirit," Says the Lord almighty. **Zechariah 4:6 (NIV)**

Always giving thanks to God the Father for everything, in the name of our Lord Jesus Christ. **Ephesians 5:20 (NIV)**

Rejoice always; pray continually; give thanks in all circumstances, for this is God's will for you in Christ Jesus. **1 Thessalonians 5:16-18 (NIV)**

But you, O LORD, are a shield about me, my glory, and the lifter of my head. **Psalm 3:3 (ESV)**

Pebbles from the Path: Motherhood

Use this section to write notes from this chapter or jot down things that come to mind from your life in the area of motherhood.

_____

_____

_____

_____

_____

_____

_____

_____

_____

_____

_____

_____

_____

_____

_____

_____

_____

_____

_____

_____

_____

_____

_____

_____

_____

_____

_____

_____

_____

_____

Putting Food in Its Place

With all my new circumstances came a new friend, really a new comforter, and it was food. When I was overwhelmed (I stayed overwhelmed), I would eat and eat some more. I was at home by myself, tired, caring for my now two kids, and my comfort was food. I was trained as a health educator. I also had my Master in Health Promotion, but none of that mattered. The weight of the world was heavy. Although I knew to turn to God, and I did it, it almost seemed superficial. I was going through the motions, and nothing was changing but my weight.

With all my new responsibilities and pressures, I went into hibernation and survival mode all wrapped into one. I was so tired from being sleep-deprived that the only energy I could mustard was to take care of my little ones. I had no energy for exercise or taking care of myself. I felt like I was in a fight for my life, and my very purpose depended on me getting this under control. So, the journey to freedom began, and I remember begging God to make it all better. He simply whispers that He would heal me, making it all better, but He said *inside out*. At that time, I didn't know what that truly meant, but it became increasingly clear as time passed. You see, God allowed all of the stuff from which I got my identity to fall away, and He began to build my true identity up in Him. Initially, my response to this falling away was depression. I think I knew it for a long time, but I didn't want to name it. It felt so big and overwhelming. I felt if I paid it attention, it would swallow me whole. I may not survive that, so instead, I pushed under a weight of unimaginable heaviness. If you could be a high-functioning depressed person, that was me. I still smiled through the pain and disappointment. I did all duties required of me, including chair a PTA program, co-lead my daughter's girl scout group, and teach children's church, all while being super sad. Between the roles of motherhood, the broken marriage, financial issues, and loss of my sense of purpose outside of my kids, I ate to get through my days. I was super sad and stuck. I was stuck doing many things I didn't prefer to do, but it was good for my children or someone else. I was lonely and didn't feel like I could climb out of this pit by myself, but everyone was too busy to help me. And although I tried to pretend everything was ok, I think people knew and wanted no part of it or me. I think people saw me as unfriendly because you need money to do everything. At the time, we struggled financially, so people would stop asking after the first couple of nos. It was a lonely time, but I had to get a handle on food and my well-being, so I never gave up trying. What kept me moving forward was the fact I wanted a better life for my babies. I also couldn't bear the idea of standing before the Lord with all that He had downloaded in me without making progress for the Kingdom. I had to figure it out, and the only way that was happening with all I had going on was to turn to God, cast my cares, and press into Him and His ways. As I mentioned before, I was depressed, and only God could set me free. To take the edge off of the pain, I would eat, which would give me a little relief. What I had to learn to do is abide and replace eating with praying. Spending time in worship was essential for me as well. It's during this time God pointed out that this was a Spiritual battle.

As you know, a Spiritual battle cannot be fought or won with physical weapons. Unfortunately, all that education was useless, at least at this point in the journey. I had to seek God with every ounce that I could muster. God's Word yet again became life to me. Abiding and resting in God began to heal me inside out. Rest is an unexpected weapon! Without rest, confessing God's word, praying, and worshipping God, there would not be a story to tell. Other key insights that made a difference were encouraging myself in the Lord, giving thanks, and learning about the role of rejection. There were times I felt rejected by my husband, family, church members, and even random people. Rejection by my husband, real or imagined, would set me in a tailspin of eating whatever I could get my hands on and just walking in a cloud of sadness. However, God often uses rejection to bring you to your place of purpose once you learn how to lean into Him no matter what you feel like and began to strengthen yourself with His Word. I realized that He had to be my number one, my everything. Life becomes more pleasurable when you are dancing for an audience of one, The One.

Putting food in its place is no easy feat when you are dealing with so much. What works for one may not work for the other, but being led by God must be your priority. For me, self-motivation worked when I didn't have competing priorities. When I didn't have the weight of the world on my shoulders while carrying a baby on my hip as the other one pulled at my leg. Even sometimes, with competing priorities, methods would work for a while but never lasted with all the juggling I participated in regularly. However, I propose an inner motivation that comes from within that can produce lasting results. And that internal motivation is the Holy Spirit. It is amazing the strength and guidance you can gain when you ask the Holy Spirit to get involved. The more time you spend with Him, the more He ministers to you, and you begin to heal inside out.

My starting place was getting to know the Holy Spirit as my comforter instead of food. The only way to win the spiritual battle of putting food in its place when it has become your only relief from the cares and heaviness of this world is to cry out to the Holy Spirit to give you the strength. You have to resist satan's plan for your destruction, submit to God's way of doing things, satan will then flee, and you will rise victorious even if it takes some time. Exploring the right combination of key elements will help many make that necessary turn that produces lasting results. However, the way out for me didn't begin with meal planning, scheduling exercise, and starving myself. It came by getting to know my Savior, and then He showed me the way of escape.

Journey to Wellness

Once you know whose you are and who you are, you take care of your mind, body, and soul differently than before. You are a new creation. All the old ways of doing things die. We must learn the ways of the Kingdom of God now. Changing your perspective will assist you on your journey to divine wellness.

I know about wellness. However, that meant absolutely nothing when I became a mom. I knew a lot of information about how to be healthy. I also had the skill and even supports, but my behaviors were not changing. I found out this theory didn't take into account my juggling priorities. Now that my little ones aren't so little anymore, it was time for me to get back to what I know. My perspective had to change with the help of the Holy Spirit. To be at my best and become all God created me to be, I needed my body to be healthy. I could not only depend on natural means to make a difference. I had to access spiritual means as well. The Holy Spirit had to not only become my comforter but my guide on my journey to wellness. Food had to become medicine, exercise had to become a tool, and rest had to become a weapon, all used to get me to my purpose.

I remember a time I felt a need to fast. At first, I thought it was the partial fast my family and I used to do together. For a season, the first three days out of the month, we would do a partial fast together. The partial fast was more for health reasons than spiritual and consisted of fruits, vegetables, nuts, seeds, water, and sometimes beans. We would not eat meat, sugar, or grains. It was a blessing because it would always reign my eating back in, and I loved the fact we were doing it together.

However, in my current season, restricting certain foods wasn't as easy because I had to eat what was available. When I would reach out to God for help to get my weight under control, fasting kept coming up. One day, I was on YouTube, and I came across a different kind of fasting called intermittent fasting. It resonated with me, and I began to research it more until I decided to give it a try. My 40th birthday was coming up, and I needed to shed some pounds. I decided to do the 16:8 method, which was to fast sixteen hours and eat eight hours. The best thing about the sixteen hours was that I did most of that while sleeping. I would stop eating around 8 pm and start eating around noon.

The first three days were a beast. You see, I had gotten to a place that I didn't let myself get hungry. As soon as I would feel the slightest urge, I would fill it. To get through the initial days, I stayed on the couch in and out of sleep. My body was like, what's up? However, on the fourth day, I happen to be at school volunteering. I didn't get to eat until after seventeen hours of fasting, and I was ok. I felt like I had broken through to the other side. With the fasting and no other real dietary changes except lowering my sugar intake (no coffee every day) and no exercise, I lost six pounds in about a month. I now can go a reasonable length of time without eating, and I don't get the nagging headaches and nausea. It helps me to stop and think before I eat. I still enjoy food, and I don't fast every day, but it is a part of my routine because it checks my eating in a way nothing else has been able to. Intermittent fasting may not be for you because no two journeys will be alike, but I encourage you to access your current state and ask God for guidance about your journey to wellness.

Again, remember that many times it is more than a physical battle. Trying to force a regimen of behavior changes without seeking God's guidance for any root causes can lead to frustration and disappointment. He knows you best! Seek Him and pray about the changes you may need to make and ask the Holy Spirit to help you. You will be amazed at how He truly is your helper!

When you do get to behavior change, it is sometimes easier to add healthy behaviors at first instead of trying to take away unhealthier actions. For example, drink more water, get more sleep, eat more vegetables and fruit instead of restricting foods and behaviors. Over time, you will be encouraged to let the unhealthy behaviors go, and soon you too will be on your own journey to wellness. Here you will find some general suggestions to pray about and research for yourself.

Ideas to Daily Detox

- Lemon water first thing in the morning
- Oil Pulling
- Salt Water Flush
- Drink Adequate Water
- Epsom Salt Baths and Foot Soaks
- Intermittent Fasting
- Lymphatic Stimulation (dry brushing, rebounder)

Ideas to Build up Your Body (See Sow These Seeds and Reap a Harvest of Health below)

- Fruits & Vegetables
- Grass-Fed Organic Meats
- Probiotics
- Enzymes
- Magnesium Oil
- Essential Oils

- Fermented Foods & Drinks (Apple Cider Vinegar with Mother, Sauerkraut, Kefir, & Kombucha)
- Other Supplements to Research: Royal Jelly/Bee Pollen/Propolis, Turmeric/Black Pepper, Nettle Leaf, Ginger, Quercetin/Bromelain, Raw Food Multivitamin

Visit www.seedsthatlast.com to learn more about these health topics.

Please remember this information is for educational purposes only.

Sow these seeds and reap a harvest of health!

Eliminate Hydrogenated Oils – I call hydrogenated fats bad or fake fats. Hydrogenated oils are man-made oils made to extend the shelf-life of many foods found in grocery stores. However, this man-made oil is horrible for your health, and studies have shown that it increases your bad cholesterol, decreases your good cholesterol, and causes heart disease. It is important to identify foods that you consume that have hydrogenated oils (also known as trans fats) and work to eliminate these harmful, unhealthy oils. Always check your ingredients list for the words hydrogenated or partially hydrogenated oils. Although the front of the package may say no trans fats, if the ingredients list hydrogenated oils, stay away.

Eliminate Artificial Sweeteners – I believe the name says it best why we should stay away. The word "artificial" should alert you. I cannot stress enough to stay away from processed foods or foods made in a lab. Whole foods are the way to go. Some artificial sweeteners are linked to cancer, while others are neurotoxins. If you have used artificial sweeteners for health reasons in the past, replace artificial sweeteners with stevia. Stevia is a natural alternative with no calories and does not adversely affect your blood sugar. Omit artificial sweeteners (aspartame, saccharin, sucralose) and replace them with natural sweeteners (stevia, sucanat, honey, maple syrup, etc.).

Eliminate High Fructose Corn Syrup – High Fructose Corn Syrup is a man-made sweetener made many times with genetically modified enzymes and corn. It is used to increase shelf life. It's cheaper, so many food manufacturers use it instead of sugar or natural sweeteners. It's best to eliminate this sweetener from your diet by only consuming foods and drinks with natural sweeteners.

Reduce Sugar –Many times, you hear sugar referred to as "empty calories" because sugar has calories but no nutrients. Although sugar is "natural," it has been processed and stripped of most of its nutrients. Additionally, sugar in large amounts is very unhealthy. Sugar has been known to suppress the immune system, and it contributes to being overweight and obese. It is best to limit your intake of sugar. Make sure to read labels because lots of foods have hidden amounts of sugar in them.

Increase Whole Foods — Eating a diet of whole foods is especially important when dealing with a body that is out of alignment. Whole foods include whole grains (ancient grains are the best.), legumes, fruits, and vegetables. Fruits and vegetables have so many nutrients in them; they could be considered medicine. Try to eat 5 to 9 servings a day of a variety of brightly colored fruits and vegetables. Also, make sure you are eating some of your fruits and vegetables raw. The more you eat raw, the better. You may think 5 to 9 servings is a lot, but it is not when you consider 1 cup of lettuce (the greener the better) is one serving, and so is a small orange. Include fruits and vegetables during your snacks, and you will be well on your way to your 5 to 9 a day.

Limit process foods that are generally unhealthy and packed with salt as well as other preservatives. Be mindful of the choices you make when it comes to meat. Choose healthy meats (lean beef, chicken, turkey, and fish) and watch your portions.

The Easy Way

If you reduce the processed foods in your diet, you will limit hydrogenated oils, high fructose corn syrup, excess sugar, artificial sweeteners, and many other harmful food additives.

He Restores My Soul

If God felt it was important to rest and restore on the 7th day, we should too. Our bodies and minds are regularly called on to perform, and for them to perform their best, they must have rest. Try to get seven to eight hours of sleep a night and begin honoring the Sabbath. Quiet your mind to give it a break. Have times when you just say no to technology. Rest is an unexpected weapon that prepares you for your journey.

Going Upstream

If I am honest, stress is something I still battle. It is so tricky because I became so accustomed to it. Many times, I didn't realize that I was even stressed. That anxious state became my norm and was the background of my life story. I think it began with desiring to control my life at an early age. I became fixated on fixing everything wrong in hopes of enjoying stability, safety, and peace. However, we live in a fallen world, and that which I was desperately seeking is hard to come by, at least in the way that I had envisioned.

Life experience, God's word, and helpful advice from the wise began to help me see the light at the end of the tunnel. I realized that I always tried to fix the symptoms and not get to the issues' roots. I needed to go upstream and deal with my thinking. The tricky thing about this is it takes real work to capture your thoughts and bring them under submission to the Word of God.

Through my research, I realized that some of my common practices had a name like rumination. Rumination is when I would think about something I said or that had happened to me over and over again. I had learned to fixate on fixing everything. However, that left little to no room for thinking on what was lovely and a good report. I asked God for true freedom, so He began to move things around. Wounds and issues rose to the surface. Although painful, this process was needed to align my thoughts to His. Lies that held strongholds together for years were being revealed. Slowly, I began to glimpse the freedom that was promised to me. The Bible does say the truth shall set you free. So as the truth of God's Word was shined on my thoughts and thinking patterns, my mind started to be renewed. I no longer had to believe the lie that it was just my nature to be anxious, or because of childhood circumstances, I was stuck. When I accepted Christ into my life, I became a new creation, and God was revealing my new nature and teaching me to walk it out with Him.

Buster's Words of Wisdom

Years ago, I became interested in my family history, and this interest led me to seek out key family members to learn all they knew about our family. During this search, I developed a wonderful relationship with my Uncle Buster. Uncle Buster was my great uncle, one of my Maw Maw's younger siblings. I would call and check on him. He would always tell me family stories, a few jokes, and wisdom from his life experience. One day out of the blue, he began telling me about the useless nature of worry. You see, he loved being outside and hunting, and many of his stories would come from those experiences. He said, "you never see a bird worrying. Some people worry all the time, but the worry is like a record playing on a record player. Your mind goes round and round about something. Before the current record stops, you go to the shelf and pick up another record to go around, but it is pointless. Just like rocking in a rocking chair takes you nowhere, neither does the spinning of worries in your head." I am not sure if he knew he was encouraging me that day, but he was. I will forever be grateful for our relationship. I am so thankful for that time. A desire to learn more about our family's history fostered some amazing relationships I may have otherwise not had the privilege to experience. My Uncle Buster has since then gone home. He left months after my Maw Maw did, but he will never be forgotten. This lesson and many others will continue to inspire a love for life he always exhibited.

Other revelations that were instrumental in me seeing life and my circumstances were seeing God in the situation with me, changing my perspective, and living in the moment. The Word of God says we will be in perfect peace when our mind stays on Jesus (Isaiah 26:3). It really works. I would even envision Jesus with me in difficult situations, and it would help me relax. Things could be hard, but with Jesus by your side, He is all you need.

Perspective is important as well. Being grateful is one of the best ways to change your perspective. Focusing on what you are thankful for daily is a wise practice. I also was able to gain a proper perspective when I would ask myself, is this a life matter or eternity matter. If it is an eternity matter (something that would keep me out of Heaven), amp up your stress and take care of it. However, if it is just a life matter, take it down a notch. Most life matters work themselves out or at least can be figured out.

Living in the moment is also a useful tool. For me, most things I worried about were in the future or sometimes even in the past. However, most of my present moments were good, and I missed them worrying about something that may never even happen. I would say, "Do I have manna for the day?" If yes, which I can't remember a time it was no, I would work to shelf that concern. The Word of God also instructs us to do that with the scripture Matthew 6:25-34 (NIV)...

"Therefore, I tell you, do not worry about your life, what you will eat or drink; or about your body, what you will wear. Is not life more than food, and the body more than clothes? Look at the birds of the air; they do not sow or reap or store away in barns, and yet your heavenly Father feeds them. Are you not much more valuable than they? Can any one of you by worrying add a single hour to your life?

"And why do you worry about clothes? See how the flowers of the field grow. They do not labor or spin. Yet I tell you that not even Solomon in all his splendor was dressed like one of these. If that is how God clothes the grass of the field, which is here today and tomorrow is thrown into the fire, will He not much more clothe you— you of little faith? So do not worry, saying, 'What shall we eat?' or 'What shall we drink?' or 'What shall we wear?' For the pagans run after all these things, and your heavenly Father knows that you need them. But seek first His Kingdom and His righteousness, and all these things will be given to you as well. Therefore, do not worry about tomorrow, for tomorrow will worry about itself. Each day has enough trouble of its own.

A little note about dinnertime...

After giving 132%, I dreaded dinner times. Don't let people throw shade because that's not your thing. I am sure you can run circles around them with the gifts God gave you. Your focus is to make dinnertime work for your family. Praise God my husband loves to cook, another gift from God. When I am left to cook, I am all about what I affectionately call "quick cooks." They are nutritious, delicious, and most of all, quick! Some of my favorite "quick cooks" include potato bowls, breakfast for dinner, chicken wraps, veggie soup, and chili. I like these options because you can add veggies and no thaw time. Hurray!

Visit the website for "Quick Cook" recipes and other ideas for making dinnertime work for your family.

Please remember this information is for educational purposes only.

Made to Move

We, as human beings, have gotten good at perverting the purpose of things. Most of the time when you think of exercise, you think of a sexy body, tight glutes, firm arms, and flat abs, or for a long time, that is what I thought. For many years my motivation for exercise was to look good for myself and especially look good to others. I would say health was a reason sometimes when I was feeling noble, but the truth was it was all about the looks. I remember exercising for hours when I was in college. Although I was a nice size, I looked in the mirror and desired to be thinner. It is funny how we change. After the stress of grad school, my job, and two babies, I would take that number easily that I so frequently tried to drive down.

Exercise had always meant a better me, a more accepted me until it would not work for me anymore. It wouldn't work either because I was overeating to deal with stress or too busy to exercise at all. It was not until later, when trying to relieve myself from stress-induced back pain, that I realized we were made to move. At this time, physical activity began to mean more to me than it had ever in the past.

The revelation began with physical therapy when my therapist talked of how my hips were rotated. This rotation slightly made one leg look shorter than the other when she was examining me. She would work on stretching me out and loosening different areas of my hip. Then my hip would rotate into place, and my legs would become even. Now you would not notice this normally, but upon close examination, it was noticeable. However, once I stretched, things lined up.

I also noticed a similar pattern while taken prenatal yoga when I was pregnant with my second child. Because I moved my body in ways that generally I didn't do on a day-to-day basis, it made my body feel stronger. By the end of a 45-minute session, I could sit on the floor cross-legged without the pain I experience in that same position at the beginning of the class. What I started to realize and understand in a way I never understood is that we are made to move. It doesn't have to be elaborate or choreographed, but movement nonetheless.

While I now know that moving my body is good for more than just good looks, I have different responsibilities.

Although I know the importance of movement, when I put it next to caring for a child, cooking a meal, getting some sleep, it always manages to slide down the list. What next? It looks like I need a new perspective. Just like with nutrition taking care of your body is more than physical. To be and do all God has called you to be, you need your physical body to be healthy. This makes physical activity a priority and not a luxury. Ask God to help you get motivated and find something you can enjoy. I love walking with a friend and dancing. I am most consistent when I know someone else is counting on me, and it is enjoyable because it goes by fast because of the conversation.

However, I must say walking alone has its benefits as well. That is one of my times that I get to quiet my mind and hear from the Lord. He gives me lots of food for thought. I like to call it pebbles on the path (that is why you see those sections throughout this book). Just like when you were a kid, and you would come back with rocks you collected from your outside excursions. God gives you wisdom that you can collect from your journey. So, I must say both walking with others and alone both have their benefits and are worth trying.

Overall, I think it is really important to do something you enjoy if you plan on staying consistent. If you get out of the routine, just start it back up and be mindful of negative self-talk. Many times, I would find myself not doing anything when I couldn't do a lot because of negative self-talk. Quiet that quickly and know that just moving your body is a great benefit for your spirit, soul, and body. Anything you do to take care of your temple is beneficial and worth the effort and the time.

Just Get Moving

Moving your body is essential. Work your way up to at least 30 minutes of activity on most days of the week. Walking is an excellent form of physical activity that most people can do in most places. You can also take 10-minute praise breaks throughout the day. Praise breaks are great for turning your attention back to God and getting your body moving. In addition, try to do some strength training moves like planks, push-ups, squats, lunges, etc.). You also want to find times to stretch. Carving out times in the morning and evening to stretch and pray allows you to incorporate two very important things in your life daily.

Please remember this information is for educational purposes only.

Scripture for the Journey: Wellness

Lord, your discipline is good, for it leads to life and health. You restore my health and allow me to live. **Isaiah 38:16 (NLT)**

I have set the Lord always before me; because He is at my right hand, I shall not be shaken. **Psalm 16:8-9 (ESV)**

So humble yourselves before God. Resist the devil and he will flee from you. Come close to God, and God will come close to you. **James 4:7-8 (NLT)**

But the Comforter, which is the Holy Ghost, whom the Father will send in my name, He shall teach you all things, and bring all things to your remembrance, whatsoever I have said unto you. **John 14:26 (KJV)**

This is what the Sovereign Lord, the Holy One of Israel, says: "Only in returning to me and resting in Me will be saved. In quietness and confidence is your strength. But you would have none of it. **Isaiah 30:15 (NLT)**

Casting down imaginations, and every high thing that exalteth itself against the knowledge of God, & bringing into captivity every thought to the obedience of Christ. **2 Corinthians 10:5 (KJV)**

Finally, brothers and sisters, whatever is true, whatever is noble, whatever is right, whatever is pure, whatever is lovely, whatever is admirable – if anything is excellent or praiseworthy – think about such things. Whatever you have learned or received or heard from me, or seen in me – put it into practice. And the God of peace will be with you. **Philippians 4:8-9 (NIV)**

Jesus said to the people who believed in Him, "you are truly my disciples if you remain faithful to my teachings. And you will know the truth and the truth will set you free." **John 8:31 (NLT)**

Let us, therefore, come boldly to the throne of grace, that we may obtain mercy and find grace to help in time of need. **Hebrews 4:16 (NKJV)**

Pebbles from the Path: Wellness

Use this section to write notes from this chapter or jot down things that come to mind from your life in the area of wellness.

_____

_____

_____

_____

_____

_____

_____

_____

_____

_____

_____

_____

_____

_____

_____

_____

_____

_____

_____

_____

_____

_____

_____

_____

_____

_____

_____

Unapologetically Who God Created Me to Be

I love that God teaches us in the way that we should go. Every season of our life, we are being taught something. Unfortunately, we get so busy that we must be pre-tested eight times before we realize we are even being taught anything. I have known God for a while now. I can remember feeling like my life was uneventful, and I didn't have a testimony. I had no real test to talk about. Well, things change, and life happens. And now I can say I have had a "few" tests here and there that God has used and is using to grow me. As I look back, it is astonishing how you can see His loving hand guiding you in each test and each season as you learn more of His way of doing life. Although some tests and seasons are difficult, looking back at what He has done in my life assures me that 1. This too shall pass 2. He loves me and wants the best for me 3. He will never leave me or forsake me, and 4. He is committed to helping me know who He truly is, so I can know who I am in Him.

Identity is a foundational piece that affects many aspects of our life. You must know who you are and walk confidently in that to be all you were created to be. With this being true, you can understand why many times elements of our identity are attacked very young, and we grow up seeking a wide range of things to feel that void. I like to call these identity stealers. They come in many forms; money, position, privilege, degrees, possessions, and the list goes on and on. When we have these things will feel like somebody. The hole doesn't feel so vast. As long as those things stay in place, we never become all that God created us to be. We don't get to know all He can be for us. We don't need to because we made it. Right? However, for many years my prayer was, *God help me to be all you created me to be*. Through my life circumstances, He was committed to answering that prayer.

I grew up as the middle child of five. My mom worked hard, very hard. My father wasn't there, but I did have a stepfather. However, I always longed for a daddy. I longed for someone to protect me, someone who always had my best interest in mind, someone to shield life's problems, someone whose lap I could find refuge. Instead, the load was too much for one woman to shoulder, so we had to help bear the load, and it was heavy, especially for a child. When you add sisters looking for their identity and finding it in all the wrong places, it gets tricky. I was singled out because of my skin color and shape. It was hard, and I felt out of place and invisible until 6th grade. I started making straight A's. I receive lots of attention and praise. For the first time, I felt like somebody, and I wasn't going to give that up. I worked very hard for my grades. No one had to push me, for I pushed myself. I remember getting to high school and getting a 92, a B at the time, and I was devastated. However, I realized after all those years of feeling out of place, invisible, and without control, I could have control over my grades. I would work hard, go to college, have money, buy nice things, and live a nice life. I was ready to make it happen for me while still praying to God to help me be all He created me to be. Little did I know that simple prayer was going to turn my nice life upside down.

So, I began my journey of performing, and I must say I did it well. But God loved me too much to leave me there. I remember being in Graduate School. I was in the middle of doing the program for my Master's Project. I was in this huge church with no one in sight. I was expecting the participants soon, and I couldn't find anyone to assist me. I was in a place of a meltdown when I looked behind me. Behind me in the bookstore window was a big poster that jumped out at me, and it read…*"I am the vine; you are the branches. If you remain in me and I in you, you will bear much fruit; apart from me, you can do nothing." John 15:5 (NIV)*

Over the next years, He was going to teach me exactly what that scripture meant through experience. I had learned to do life in my own strength, and God was on a mission to show me

"…Not by might, nor by power but My Spirit, says the Lord Almighty." Zechariah 4:6(NIV)

Surrender

And so, it continued. There was a time when I felt God saying surrender, and I look down to see the trash blowing in the wind. It looked painful. The trash was hitting up against everything that wouldn't move. This was what surrender felt like to me, but He said no lookup, and high in the sky, I saw this huge bird riding the waves of the wind so free and at peace. He said that's surrender. This is the same time He gave me the title of this book Your Purpose Depends on It! At the time, I that it was a tag line for some consulting work I wanted to do, but now I realize it was much more. It was **SURRENDER BECAUSE YOUR PURPOSE DEPENDS ON IT**!

Years passed, and I was in the process of the reluctant surrender. God knows exactly how to get you there. Through a series of life circumstances, my gripe began to weaken. I had no other choice but to surrender. It was surrender or be swallowed by the cares of this world. I slowly chose to surrender.

Later, I started learning about my identity in Christ. I bought a lot of books and studied. I began the process that was a foundational piece to my journey. At this time, I could say I learned who I was in Christ, but I didn't fully understand, nor did it become truly meaningful to me until years later. I realized not only do I have to know what the Bible says about me, but I must also believe it by practicing my new identity. I begin to get the practical steps I needed to make the changes I so desperately desired.

"Very truly I tell you, unless a kernel of wheat falls to the ground and dies, it remains only a single seed. But if it dies, it produces many seeds." John 12:24(NIV)

Get Ready

While studying brokenness, I saw it differently for the first time. Brokenness is necessary, and it allows you to access God's power. One morning during my devotion, I felt like I needed a word from God because I was going through so much. It was Sunday, and I remember thinking maybe I will get a word when I get to church. This particular weekend I was babysitting my niece, and her mom was picking her up before church. When my sister arrived, she said as she was driving down the road, God gave her a word for me that was really strong. She got my attention! She preceded to share the word.

> *"Be still for the outpouring of My Spirit."*
> *She said the word BIG keeps coming to*
> *mind and to brace myself because it is so*
> *much. She told me to speak life to all the*
> *devil tried to take from me because God*
> *favors me."*

Thank you, God. That was quick, but what does it mean. I felt like I needed to stay low and stay at His feet, and I will be ok. I felt like surrender, trust, & wait was my game plan. While sharing this with my cousin, she shared that a part of waiting was serving. I could do that, I thought. I could serve while I waited. I would sow seeds right where I was in that season of my life. One of the areas I was serving in was the Children's Church. About a week later, I was preparing for the Children's Church lesson. It was a lesson on Jesus being tempted (Matthew 3:16-17; 4:1). A summary of the story is as follows: Jesus was baptized. The Spirit of God descended on Him. God says He is pleased, and then the Spirit leads Jesus into the wilderness where the devil tempted Him. Jesus used the Word of God to resist the devil, and the devil went away. Then angels came to minister to Jesus, and Jesus began His ministry. I thought, wow, this seems similar to the word I got from my sister. To God, I am saying I am listening, and if that wasn't clear enough, I get to church, and my Pastor says it is Pentecost Sunday. He goes on to explain exactly what that means. In a nutshell, Jesus had told the disciples to go and wait for the Spirit to fall on them, and then they would receive the power to do their ministry. I think that God was trying to tell me something. Could I be close to the other side? Could the brokenness that I have experienced be yielding God's power in my life shortly? Is it now time for the ministry God has placed in me to take off? I wasn't sure, but He impressed upon me that if I kept my eyes on Him, I would walk on water. While listening to a minister, God further confirmed this possibility. It's amazing how God would speak something to me, and I would hear it multiple places. God speaks. He is not trying to hide anything from you. If we take the time to seek Him and spend time in His presence, He will guide us. It is amazing how He gets our attention and confirms the message from numerous unrelated places. Oh, How I love Him so.

> **Call to me and I'll answer you, and will tell you about great and hidden things that you don't know. Jeremiah 33:3 (NIV)**

Still in the Wilderness, but I see Grapes

Three years later, I was still in the wilderness, but I still believed in God for relief. As I said before, I started to listen to messages daily. The word I received from God through these messages was life-changing. It took me to another level of understanding Kingdom principles and God's way of life. A lot of the teachings challenged me to see my difficulties differently and to understand who God was in each circumstance. The teachings encouraged me to spend quality time with the Lord, meditating on truths, and communicating with Him in a new way. One day I was inspired to try out a new way of praying that encourages you to listen to what God drops in your spirit and meditate on that. The Scripture that God gave me, and I confessed over and over was *No eye has seen, no ear has heard, and no mind has imagined what God has prepared for those who love Him. 1 Corinthians 2:9 (NLT)*

I was trying so hard to pass the test because I was tired of being without what I thought I needed. One day I was so frustrated I decided I was just going to relax. I planned on watching a movie and having a latté. I will get back to praying and confessing after a break. I randomly picked an unfamiliar movie on Netflix that seemed light and could help me forget about life for an hour. It looked like a light love story, just perfect for what I needed. About halfway through, I noticed they briefly focused on scripture, and I thought that is interesting. I jotted the scripture down, thinking that it could be useful for a meeting I had previously. At the end of the movie, the main character was experiencing some difficulties, and a family friend handed her a paper, and it read.

> *"Don't lose yourself in the temporary*
>
> *No one has ever seen*
>
> *No one has ever heard &*
>
> *No one has imagined*
>
> *What God has prepared."*
>
> *Scripture Quoted in the Movie "Coffee Shop"*

I was blown away. The movie didn't present itself as a Christian movie, yet the very scripture that God had put on my heart just so happen to be quoted on a day that I really needed it. I serve a loving God.

Fear Not

I usually use my phone or some electronic device for my devotion, but for some reason, I had my physical Bible this time. I was sitting at the kitchen table with my Bible, and I just cried out to God to help me not be fearful. I was tired of being fearful. I opened the Bible, and it opened to Isaiah 43. Here are some of the highlights.

But now, this is what the Lord says—
He who created you, O Jacob, He who
formed you, O Israel: "Fear Not, for I have
redeemed you; I have summoned you
by name; you are mine. When you pass
through the waters, I will be with you; and
when you pass through the rivers, they
will not sweep over you. When you walk
through the fire, you will not be burned;
the flames will not set you ablaze. For I am
the Lord, Your God, the Holy One of Israel,
your Savior; I give Egypt for your ransom,
Cush, and Seba in your stead. Since you
are precious and honored in my sight,
and because I love you, I will give men in
exchange for you, and people in exchange
for your life. Do not be afraid, for I am with
you; Isaiah 43:1-5 (NIV)

"You are my witnesses, "declares the Lord,
"and my servant whom I have chosen, so
that you may know and believe me and
understand that I am He. Before me no
god was formed, nor will there be one
after me. I, even I, am the Lord and apart
from me, there is no savior. I have revealed
and proclaimed—I, am not some foreign
god among you. You are my witnesses,
"declares the Lord, "that I am God. Yes,

and from ancient days I am He. No one can deliver out of my hand. When I act, who can reverse?" Isaiah 43:10-13 (NIV)

Forget the former things; do not dwell on the past. See, I am doing a new thing! Now it springs up; do you not perceive it? I am making a way in the desert and streams in the wasteland." Isaiah 43:18-19 (NIV)

This experience showed me that God is with me. He loves and He hears me. He is concerned with the details of my life.

Season of Devotion

Before kids, lengthy devotions and worship times were a regular part of my life. It gave me the strength to do the hard things and relieved me of daily stresses. Since then, my devotions have gotten shorter, and worship tends to be quick praise breaks. However, in this season, I learned that the refueling that happens with devotion and praise is undeniable.

One Sunday after church, Pastor sent for me because he had a word for me. My Pastor's Word for me that day was...

"Seek first the Kingdom of God, and His righteousness; and all these things shall be added unto you (Matthew 6:33)." He went on to say that your children are getting older, and this will allow you time to get back to the way you used to do your devotions. He said, "don't worry about anything. God will take care of your children, your marriage, and your finances." I was amazed because not only did I have a promise to hold on to, but my Pastor knew nothing of my devotional life before my kids. I will say again, God speaks. He speaks through His word, a still small voice (a knowing), and through others. We just have to be still enough to listen. This promise that my Pastor spoke over me kept me through long, difficult seasons. Seasons that seemed to never end, but I hoped and trusted in God's promise to me. Believing that God knows, He sees, and He is taking care of the things that concern me.

Season of Trusting

Going from two incomes to one is no joke and not for the faint at heart. However, my husband and I felt clear that we wanted to be the ones to train our kids up. We felt like it was God's desire for our family, and we heard it pays off in dividends. God used this time to build trust as well as the time I had to send them to school. The great thing is that a wise friend once told me that God would honor our sacrifice, and that seems to be coming true more and more day by day. This season has seemed especially long, and it may be due to the fact I didn't incorporate previously learned lessons. I prayed many prayers of fear and not faith, but I am so thankful for God's patience with me. I am remembering the lessons and putting them into practice. In this season, I learned, and I am still learning to trust in Him fully.

Write it Down and Make it Plain

Many times, God gives us the desires of our hearts, but we miss it with all our competing interests. It is faith-building to watch Him while He works on your behalf. I encourage you to write down and date what God is doing and saying to you, so you can see how He works and is intricately involved in your life.

At one point, my mom impressed upon me to make a list of the things I was trusting God to do in my life. I made a large print of it and placed it on the wall in my closet. At the top, it read, "Ask and it will be given to your; seek and you will find; knock and the door will be opened to you." (Matthew 7:7 NIV) I had dated it in November 2019. By the end of January 2020, the first one was answered. By the end of January 2021, the second one was answered. Neither one of these items was simple to answer, or so I thought. I must say, seeing that He answered the first gave me faith for all the other ones listed. It is also interesting to see how He answered the prayers. It was totally different than any answer I had imagined, but it was perfect. I am not a big journal writer, but I am a note-taker. I constantly jot down what I feel God is saying to me. It is amazing the kind of relationship you can have with the Creator of it all, your Father, if you are willing to write it all down.

Many times, what we seek cannot be found in religion because it only comes from relationship. God wants a relationship with **YOU**! Don't let anyone tell you differently. For me, that saying "I know too much about Him to ever doubt Him" (Unknown) rings true here. I have too many experiences under my belt to ever believe that God's desire for me is religion over relationship, and jotting my life notes down is our story together. As I mentioned, it has not only increased my faith, but it helped me learn more about Him. It has also help me to learn more about who I am in Him. Writing it down truly gives you hope that you are working your way through some of the hardest times, and just like Moses, Joseph, David, and Jesus, after the wilderness comes the promised land, the provision, the placement, and the ministry.

God Is a Provider

God is a provider. He continually shows me that He is my true Source and is patient with me when I need a little reminder. One day I was becoming overwhelmed with our finances, and I felt in my spirit – Don't let your needs become distractions. If you truly believe that I provide according to my riches and glory, you will be about your Father's business. I will take care of yours. It's the same message in seeking the Kingdom first, and everything else will be added (Matthew 6:33). It is amazing how He provides and how experiencing His provision grows your faith. The answered prayer doesn't always come like you think it will come. Take a look again. Your prayer may have already been answered.

A Story of His Provision: Eighty-Three Cents and Two Offerings

What do these two things have to do with one another? This is how I started my week one Sunday. We had eighty-three cents in the bank, and we were expecting two offerings at church. You can look at this experience in two different ways. Well, give your eighty-three cents. God will multiply just like the widow and her mites, or surely the church could help you being that they are taking up two offerings in one Sunday. To be fair, no one at the church knew that this is what we had for the week. No one knew we needed lunches for the kids, gas money to get to and from work, and meals to eat at home with just eighty-three cents in the bank.

When my husband realized this reality, He said, "how can we do this? All I have is twenty dollars, and that must be used for gas to get to work". I boldly stated that God would provide and that we will just take one day at a time. I said this while completely going in and out of internal panic. You see, if we could just figure out how to make it to Wednesday, my husband could cash a check from his part-time job. It wouldn't be much since he only had a couple of days on that check, but at least it would be something. I entertained asking someone but hoped for a different solution. I got in the shower that night crying out to the

Lord between cries and finally confessions. He had to work it out. That is what He promised, so I waited.

I would love to say that this was a peaceful wait, but that really wasn't the kind of wait I experienced. I still was going in and out of internal panic until I could reign my emotions in enough to confess. So, first things first, the kids needed lunch. I found ravioli in the freezer with no sauce. I ask my husband to get some sauce. He took some coins he had by the bed to get the sauce. The kids were not super happy about their lunch, but I demanded no complaints. If they only knew what was being juggled. I get the kids to school. Thank the Lord we had enough eggs for breakfast and my lunch. In between doing work training videos. I pondered how Lord how.

Many times, I would feel like there were two entries to my cabinets. We would be out of something like soap, and I would reach to the back of the cabinet only to find one last bar of soap. I felt God had to be on the other side, restocking when needed. I thought how wonderful if I could reach to the back of this freezer, and there would be a pack of ground beef that I didn't know about or that was conveniently restocked once I reached to the back. I wasn't ready to try my chances yet, so I continued training. Later, I was standing in the kitchen, and I remembered we had two hamburgers I could use. That was it! Just like that, I could now get us through supper with chili for our meal.

Earlier I thought I should have tried to take some clothes to the kids' consignment after church, but that didn't happen. And then I went on our beloved coin search.

OK, the beloved is pushing it. I absolutely dreaded lugging coins to the bank, but this time at least I could take the kids. It will look like it is their money, which most of it was. I realized the kids had a way to help. That morning I had shared with them that it is not always easy, and my son expressed he wish he could help. I usually try to shield them, but this may be a lesson that they needed to learn.

So, while they were at school, I meticulously gather all the coins I could find, putting them in separate baggies labeled with their names. I also gathered the coins from my purse and the bedside coins. I also found 20 dollars from my daughter's piggy bank and purse. I got out a sheet of paper and entitled it IOU with the amounts that I got from each child. I also added signature lines to be signed by both parties. I was nervous. My daughter is a saver, and my son had his sights set on a new toy. What will they say? I presented to them my proposal when they got in the car from school and added that this would be a way to not eat ravioli all week but get some lunches they enjoy. And that we would return it to them on Friday when dad got paid. They agreed.

We went to the bank, and altogether the money totaled $84.60. We rushed to Aldi's to get food for the week, with a list that I had thoughtfully crafted earlier and a calculator. We had to hurry. I had to get back home, make the chili, and head to work by eight, and I wouldn't be home until after midnight. We did it! My kids were simply amazing. They handled it so well. And guess what? We made it to Wednesday! We had more food than we could eat that week, lunches, and gas. My God is faithful. And to add a cherry on top, a Bible Study book that I wanted was given to me, the day was overcast (a blessing because we had no AC in the car the entire month of JULY!), and the temperature while in the carpool line was pleasant (counting ALL my blessings).

Let me say it again. He is faithful! He showed Himself strong and made a way out of no way. It's like He kept saying, I am with you, you are fine, I am with you, you are fine. And I say to you; God is with you, you are fine. Stand back and watch Him work on your behalf, knowing that His ways are not our ways. However, He has promised to never leave us nor forsake us and to provide manna for the day, and He did just that! Oh yeah, at that time, we still had eighty-three cents in the bank. God provided for our needs without touching the bank account and before the check on Wednesday. He even added a book I didn't have to pay for. That's my God!

God Blesses Us Through Problems

One day while planting some tulips under my mailbox, I looked up at the tattered mailbox wishing that we could get a new one. However, that was not a priority at this time, so I planted my flowers and was done. Not even a week later, we woke to find a note on our door that read, "I am sorry. I was still half asleep, and we hit your mailbox. Here is our insurance information." Sure enough, our mailbox was demolished. However, when their insurance company paid us, we not only had money to get a new mailbox (something I desired), but we could get a few Christmas presents as well. I don't know if this is a thing, but I started to notice how God would bless us through what on the surface seemed like a problem.

This could not have been truer than in the year 2020 when He opened the door for a full-time position and increase during the middle of a pandemic. Both my husband and I were working from home. We didn't have to pay for childcare because the children were at home with us, and we were not spending money on gas. We were able to catch up on bills, buy needed appliances, do some home repairs, save money, and even invest. He also fulfilled a promise, which was that He would give us seed to sow.

In addition, I thought I could finally publish my book with this new income. When one company sent me 40% off the publishing, I thought this has got to be it, but God had a better plan. Around three days before a short story contest was closing from my current publisher, I saw the contest. I was able to use an excerpt from this book to submit my entry right before the contest ended. And I won! What did I win, you ask? A free publishing package to publish this book. I had been working on this book for years, wondering how I could ever get it published, and God yet again provided.

His plans are so much bigger than ours. I was overwhelmed by how God continued to bless us during the pandemic and simply humbled. God was repositioning us during this time. The times that He had spoken BIG in

2014, the words of acceleration, and putting the seed in the ground and harvest coming right up, I was living.

Striving is Not the Way

I was under the false assumption that if I wasn't worrying, playing it over in my head 1000 times, and striving, that I wasn't doing all that I could to help the situation. Slowly I am learning that striving isn't the Kingdom way. It is actually more closely associated with the world's way of doing things. I can make my request known and then rest. I can trust that God always keeps His promises. And because I belong to Him, I will lack no good thing. He makes my crooked paths straight. So, I focus my attention on getting to know Him better and let Him take care of the rest.

The Wilderness Experience

I learned valuable lessons in the wilderness. One lesson is that God speaks. However, to hear Him, we must take time to listen. When we jot down the scriptures and phrases that He gives us, we realize just how intricately He is involved. We then can ask questions and watch how He answers us, sometimes really quickly. You get to be amazed at how He loves you so much and cares about your day-to-day.

Call to me and I will answer you and tell you great unsearchable things you do not know. Jeremiah 33:3 (NIV)

I also learned that surrender is not only a prerequisite to growth but also for fulfilling your purpose. Surrender definitely takes trust. However, as you experience life with God and get to know Him better, it becomes easier to do. Many of my desires began to melt into an earnest, let it be according to Your Word. Yes, I may initially want a particular thing, but it becomes less appealing if that thing is not in God's will for my life. I actually started praying for God to remove desires that were not in His will for me. It is easier that way. When you surrender and began to do life His way, no matter what you feel, you are rewarded in ways you could have never predicted.

Submit yourselves, then, to God. Resist the devil, and he will flee from you. James 4:7 (NIV)

The wilderness increased my trust, as well. Drawing close to God and leaning on His word and promises allowed me to get to know Him better. Abiding and meditating on His word set the stage for the trust you need during wilderness seasons. Many times, during these seasons, it doesn't look right, but you can trust in His character and love for you to help see you through.

I will go before you and will level the mountains; I will break down gates of bronze and cut through bars of iron. Isaiah 45:2 (NIV)

Learning to wait well is another wilderness lesson. God's timing is perfect, and since you know Him better and trust Him more, you can be confident that what He started in you, He will finish. Now, I didn't always wait perfectly. Sometimes I was discouraged in the long waiting seasons. It is during those times I grabbed on to His word and His promises. I served where I was at and tried to remember to use what was currently in my hand. This approach helped me to get through some long seasons with some satisfaction. In addition, resting in the wait is important as well. Not only can you hear God better when you are rested, but there is also power in rest. Therefore, rest becomes key to waiting well.

Humble yourselves, therefore, under God's mighty hand, that He may lift you up in due time. Cast all your anxiety on Him because He cares for you. 1 Peter 5:6-7

And finally, it is in the wilderness where God began to heal me inside out and restore my soul. During this intimate time with Him, when He has your undivided attention, He begins to reveal His self to you. During this time, I began to recognize even more than I had before that God is my everything. He began to refine my thoughts, will, and emotions. He planted Kingdom ways of doing life into me. I was able to gain God's perspective on important life issues like looking a "problems" differently and understanding the value of being thankful. Learning that many times focusing on what you are thankful for will help you change your perspective. When you have written down your experiences with God, it also helps you see His faithfulness and makes it easier to be thankful. Repeatedly, I was reminded to live in the moment. Worrying about the past or the future isn't fruitful, and you miss the gift of today. God would remind me you are exactly where I want you to be.

The wilderness is necessary; however, it is not meant to take you out or for you to stay there. In your submission to the process, you develop muscles to believe in the impossible. A goal of the wilderness is to strengthen and prepare you for things to come. This strength and preparation are imperative for Kingdom work. In my experience, God sent hope through promises that helped me to continue to walk even when tired and overwhelmed. As we know, we continually face challenges, but we hope that through our transformation into the image of God, we become better equipped to handle the challenges in a way that builds us and propels us deeper into our purpose.

Getting to know God through experience revealed who I was in Christ and ushered me into the freedom I longed to call my own. This freedom was the backdrop of me becoming unapologetically who God had created me to be. How amazing it is to get your freedom from God, and that freedom opens you up to just be YOU. And when you unapologetically walk out who God created you to be, you walk into this sweet spot that enables what seemed like the impossible to happen with ease. God's plans are perfect. Don't fear the wilderness; embrace it! What you gain from the wilderness will far outweigh that which you are hesitant to let go of.

New Growth: More Than a Hair Journey

I *f you truly believe your identity comes from me, why is it so hard for you to cut your hair?*

When my older sister went natural, I said, "Great for you, but that just isn't me." You see, at that time, my hair was part of my identity. At any sight of "new growth," I had a touch-up (mini relaxer). My hair was shoulder-length, and I liked it. I received a lot of compliments. My hair was me, and I wasn't about to let my good thing go. I would get my hair done regularly, put on my nice clothes (I shopped a lot), and perform with the best of them.

Later, I become pregnant, and because I am a girly girl, I felt sure God was giving me a girl until I found out it was a boy. While reading a book on what God considers beautiful, it was revealed to me that I had some identity issues to work through, and I wasn't ready for my girl yet. Time past and I started playing with how long I could go before getting a relaxer. During that time, I ran across Chris Rocks' documentary "Good Hair" and decided I must figure out a way to separate myself from the relaxer. It was a relationship, an unhealthy relationship, and I remember when it began. My mom would use the straightening comb to straighten my hair when I was young, and one of our neighbors encouraged her to relax my hair. I was super excited, but I will have to admit that over the years of a burning scalp, oozing sores, hair matted to the scalp (all things we thought were normal at the time), the excitement eventually wore off.

However, I had to have straight hair, right? Of course, I did, so I bought the best flat iron and all the accessories. I commenced to keeping my hair straight with heat instead of chemicals. About ten months or so later, I had a huge problem. My beautiful straight hair that was so much a part of me was a hot mess. My hair was breaking off badly, and I couldn't figure out how to make it better, even with all the YouTube videos. I couldn't think about doing the big chop. It was intense. Had I done the wrong thing? Should I have just kept relaxing my hair no matter the consequences? I wasn't in a good place, and I just so happened to be about eight months pregnant with my baby girl. Then one day,

I was standing in the mirror in anguish, trying to figure out what to do with my hair. I was debating on whether I should do the big chop. Surely not. I told myself there has to be another way. Then this dropped in my spirit—*If you truly get your identity from Christ, why is it so hard for you to cut your hair.* You see, I had been reading books on identity, and I felt that I was good. I felt I knew that my identity came from Christ. However, the transformation was still in progress. I decided I had to prove to myself that I truly got my identity from Christ. Besides, how could I convince my new little girl that she should love how God created her if I did not love how God created me. I also encouraged myself that if I did the big chop now, it would allow me to learn what to do with my hair and gain confidence before my little girl noticed. So on December 17, 2010, I did it! I did the big chop almost a month before my baby girl was born.

Now with my new growth came "new growth." I think my family thought I was going to lose it. They swooped in the amazing way that they do with so much support and encouragement. My older sister was already natural, and around that time, both my mom and other sisters went natural. It was truly amazing the support they gave. Because it was so unlike my previous self to cut all my hair off, they rushed in with support in a big way. My mom sent me a big box of accessories that included jewelry, headbands, big earrings, and everything you could think of to equip me for my journey. My husband was supportive, which meant a lot to me. However, not everyone was supportive. This lack of support, of course, allowed me to experience more "new growth." Many people just stare at my hair. Some acted like I was part of a militant group, and others greeted me with your hair looks great instead of a simple hello. The lack of support came from all directions black and white, friend and foe. While in the post office, the lady helping me, a black woman in her 60s, could hardly help me because she was staring at my hair like she was disgusted. And then there was one lady that was kind of close to me. She would make comments like, does your husband like it? She then would talk to me about "other" people with natural hair and say it was ugly. No harm, No foul, she wasn't talking about me, right?

A turning point came when I let that same lady talk me in to straighten my hair after two years of being natural. I thought I needed it trimmed, and I would like to see it straighten. It is natural hair. You can't mess up natural hair, right? Wrong! After growing my natural hair out for two years, I had to cut a lot off due to heat damage. You see, I am pretty sure her view at the time was that natural hair was unruly and needed to be tamed. She tried to tame it with a flat iron. After I let her straighten my hair when I washed it, some of my hair curled back up, and some didn't. It was horrible, and I was devastated.

That was a very painful time for me because I realized I let others influence my identity still. But although very painful, that process was helpful because it brought me to a new place. What other people thought about me and my hair became less and less important. I began to appreciate and love what the Creator had in mind when He knitted me together. I am His Masterpiece. He looks at me and says I am good. His opinion of me slowly began to come to the forefront, and I learned to love my hair. Yes, my beautiful, big, natural hair. And now I rock it! I still get the looks and inappropriate comments at times, but whether you like my hair or not has nothing to do with me and my hair. I decided that I loved my natural hair. My hair was part of my journey to wholeness, and my purpose depended on it! Do you know what happened? Right! **NEW GROWTH**!!!

Growing My Natural Hair

Now natural hair is more common to see and more widely accepted, although you still hear some crazy stories sometimes. However, if you are thinking about it and haven't taken the plunge, I would go for it! Be patient because, for me, I had to train my hair. I still have good days and bad days. I would also say love the journey and enjoy each pit-stop to your destination. If you desire to grow it out, rosemary essential oil is your friend. As you know, I use Young Living essential oils because the quality is important to me. You can add rosemary to the shea buttercream I make or any of your hair products. You can find my favorite shea buttercream recipe at www.seedsthatlast.com. Ultimately, I am so glad I took the plunge when I did. My little girl loves her hair and has learned to appreciate how God created her.

Scripture for the Journey: Identity

So, God created man in His own image, in the image of God He created him; male and female He created them. **Genesis 1:27 (ESV)**

And God saw everything that He had made, and behold, it was very good. And there was evening and there was morning, the sixth day. **Genesis 1:31 (ESV)**

For we are God's masterpiece. He has created us anew in Christ Jesus, so we can do the good things He planned for us long ago. **Ephesians 2:10 (NLT)**

I praise you because I am fearfully and wonderfully made; your works are wonderful; I know that full well. **Psalm 139:14 (NIV)**

But whenever anyone turns to the Lord, the veil is taken away. Now the Lord is the Spirit, and where the Spirit of the Lord is, there is freedom. And we all, who with unveiled faces contemplate the Lord's glory, are being transformed into His image with ever-increasing glory, which comes from the Lord, who is the Spirit. **2 Corinthians 3:16-18 (NIV)**

"Am I now trying to win the approval of human beings, or of God? Or am I trying to please people? If I were still trying to please people, I would not be a servant of Christ. **Galatians 1:10 (NIV)**

If then you were raised with Christ, seek those things which are above, where Christ is, sitting at the right hand of God. Set your mind on things above, not on things on the earth. For you died, and your life is hidden with Christ in God. **Colossians3:1-3 (NKJV)**

When I discovered your words, I devoured them; they are my joy and my heart's delight, for I bear your name. Oh Lord God of Heaven's Armies. **Jeremiah 15:16 (NLT)**

"I am the vine, you are the branches. If a man remains in me and I in Him, He will bear much fruit; apart from me you can do nothing." **John 15:5 (NIV)**

As a man thinks in His heart, so is he. **Proverbs 23:7 (NKJV)**

So humble yourselves before God. Resist the devil, and he will flee from you. Come close to God, and God will come close to you. **James 4:7-8 (NLT)**

Therefore, if anyone is in Christ, he is a new creation; the old has gone, the new has come! **2 Corinthians 5:17 (NIV)**

And do not be conformed to this world, but be transformed by the renewing of your mind, that you may prove what *is* that good and acceptable and perfect will of God. **Romans 12:2 (NKJV)**

Yet in all these things we are more than conquerors through Him that loved us. **Romans 8:37 (NKJV)**

Pebbles from the Path: Identity

Use this section to write notes from this chapter or jot down things that come to mind from your life in the area of identity.

_____

_____

_____

_____

_____

_____

_____

_____

_____

_____

_____

_____

_____

_____

_____

_____

_____

_____

_____

_____

_____

_____

_____

_____

_____

_____

From Performing to Pretending to Purpose

A s you have read, in the early part of my life, I performed. I thought that was the way to be accepted and secure. I am thankful to God that He didn't leave me in that miserable place of striving to perform only to continually not measure up to people. People who are constantly changing and basing their views on their broken places. Even though I started out performing and fell into pretending, He is faithfully bringing me into my purpose. When everything I had built up fell away, I stayed in hiding as long as I could, only pushing my way to church or the store. This season of pretending was very lonely. I didn't have the means to perform, and pretending was draining. During this time, the truth of God's word and the connection of people that accepted me in this place continue to heal me. Although in the beginning, I tried to hide the despair that I felt, the season grew long. I became tired, which revealed the truth. I believe it is only when we can be true with ourselves and others before God that His truth can come in and heal.

I wish I can say it was a straight path to healing, but many times my resistance sent me around the mountain yet again. But ever so firmly yet patiently, God kept the truth before me. Sometimes it felt like I took one step forward and two steps back, but finally, I started making ground. As I look back on it, I almost turned around when the entrance to my purpose looked different than I had envisioned, but even then, God impressed upon me that this next move wasn't about a job. It was about my purpose.

As I continued, there were times I wanted to quit, but He continually sent word that I was on the right track. I remember crying out to Him in frustration one day on the way to work because He had given me so much with Seeds That Last (the ministry for developing resources for children and women). Still, it wasn't producing what I thought it was supposed to produce. Someone I hadn't seen in a long time visited the store and asked me how things were going. I went on to say I wasn't giving up on Seeds That Last, but it wasn't where I wanted it to be. She said very confidently, almost before I could even finish, "I hear the Holy Spirit saying, **ASK FOR MORE**." I was slightly perplexed because I thought Seeds That Last was "THE MORE." I felt like Seeds that Last was my destiny, but God began to reveal it was only part of the bigger picture. As months went by, I decided I would be brave and talk to the company about carrying my Seeds That Last resources.

Before I could do that, I received the word that they would be closing some of their brick-and-mortar stores. I still felt hopeful that Seed that Last Resources could help them bring in new customers. However, shortly after that, I found out all the brick-and-mortar stores would be closing. It was then that God started to unveil the bigger plan, which would grow into The Retreat (A Christian bookstore and more). This is where my faith walk would be taken to a new level. I began to realize that some Christians say a lot of things they do not believe in. It's easy to say you believe God is a provider, but many times the only time that can be tested is when you can't provide for yourself. It's only then that we can say it and show evidence that we believe it when there isn't a sign insight that it is the truth.

Now faith is the substance of things hope for the evidence of things not seen. Hebrews 11: 1 (KJV)

I got to strengthen my faith muscle because I felt like, and many individuals prayed and prophesied that God would provide every need concerning The Retreat. I received a lot of support for The Retreat, although, at times when I would share my vision, people's responses were discouraging. However, there came a time when I still didn't have all the answers, but I knew it was already done. It reminds me of the time I was in labor with my daughter, and they were trying to send me home. And before I could even think, I told the nurses to give me an hour. Who says that? I did. And in an hour, I was in active labor.

God has a plan, and I am His hands and feet. I trust Him to make my paths straight, remove barriers, and open doors that no man can shut. It is an exciting adventure. It isn't always comfortable, but it is exciting to partner with God to do Kingdom work. You must remember to be careful with who you share your God-sized vision with. Honestly, at times it can be hard to know when to share and when not to share. I sometimes know instantly when I have said too much, but I run straight into His arms and lay it all at His feet again. I pray, not my will, but thy will be done. There is a reason why God chose you to carry the vision, and others may not have the faith for it and could plant seeds of doubt in you. Spending time with God gets real during this time. You cannot afford to have time without constant communication with God. He is your source, and being too far from your source at any moment could have a devastating effect on the vision He gave you and your purpose.

And without faith, it is impossible to please God because anyone who comes to Him must believe that He exists and that He rewards those who earnestly seek Him. Hebrews 11:6 (NIV)

Too Tired to Pretend

I did a lot of my pretending at church. For a long time, church was the only place, that made it difficult to hide and to be invisible. I dreaded Sundays. Life was hard. The energy it took to get to church with a smile and repeatedly say I was fine, when I clearly was not, became more than I could bear. I would pour myself into ill-fitted clothes and fight with the ushers to sit in the back. It took all I had to step into the church and get to the back row and be present but not seen. There was a time that I decided to step back from church for a while and seek God.

I couldn't do life as usual, and that included the mundane routine of church attendance. Don't get me wrong; I love God. He is the only reason you can read my story on this page. However, I was also hurting, and I needed more than checking the box of my Sunday obligation. This time was important for me because I needed to press into Him. I didn't need to worry about the clothes I had on or if my hair was right. I didn't need to recite all the Bible verses correctly or remember the lines to the songs. It was messy. I had to seek God with all the strength I could muster. It was the only way I was guaranteed to make it through the next week.

I don't advocate for not going to church or being alone because that allows satan to have a hay day at times. However, for me, I did have my family constantly turning my attention to God. I think that was important for me because I had a pretty good relationship with God.

However, it may not have worked if my relationship with Him was not as strong. My desire for my kids to be in the church was another driving factor, and so I would push.

As I continued, my ability to pretend was being comprised, and I hated that. I liked believing that I was strong and capable of doing my life, but all of the brokenness was falling out under the weight of despair. However, it was a good thing that pretending was becoming too hard so that I could fully submit to the work God was doing in me and move on to my purpose. It was lonely and intense, but He NEVER left me alone. The best thing is that I got to know Him as My Comforter.

Although this season of pretending was lonely, and I felt invisible at times, I have a different perspective of it now. Then I wrestled with people's seemingly lack of concern and behaviors that seemed against me. It was hard not to be included and feeling forgotten. There were times that even my close family was too busy to endure. However, this was by design. And although it wasn't a place that I enjoyed, my view of it now is different. That season of my life reminds me of the times when you are pregnant. People can say kind words, buy things you may need, but ultimately when it comes to having the baby, you are the only one who can do it. And it's not something you can back out of. Once the baby is in, it must come out, and there isn't any way for that to happen except for labor. You must labor, and you must labor "alone." During this season, I had to labor, and I had to labor alone. Yes, people were all around me, but there were limits on how they could help.

I had to depend on God, and I had to learn to encourage myself like David.

> **And David was greatly distressed**; for the people spake of stoning him, because the soul of all the people was grieved, every man for his sons and for his daughters; **but David encouraged himself in the Lord His God. 1 Samuel 30:6 (KJV)**

Learning to encourage myself in the Lord during difficult times built me up and prepared me to carry out that which God placed in me. It is a necessary skill that we all must learn. And having this perspective is definitely a better way to look at it because otherwise, you could become mad and bitter. You could feel like people are too busy to care. However, if you can endure to the point of learning to encourage yourself, it is freeing. And it puts you right where God wants you to be, perfectly placed to move to the next level.

Snowy Beach Trip

I am amazed at how God can use just about anything to teach us His ways. The day that I said yes to a beach trip in January was no different. This trip was so unlike me. I still scratch my head in wonder. I am not typically the one you would call a risk-taker. However, as I journey with God, that is changing day by day. On this particular occasion, I took a risk, and I was on my way to the beach after a snowstorm. Yes, I said it! A snowstorm! I am still not sure if we should have done it but thank God for keeping us safe. And since He had my undivided attention, He began to speak.

On the way there, I was reading a magazine to keep my mind off the road. The magazine talked about how in Japan, when certain dishes were broken, they would mend the dishes back together with gold. The new mended piece would become more valuable than before. I thought that was a remarkable story. I tucked it away as a feel-good piece, but God had other plans.

When we got to the beach house safely, we decided to wrap up and walk down to the beach. We were staying in a beautiful beachfront home. It seemed like the thing to do. Although the snow was on the ground and we could slide down to the water on the ice. When we got to the beach, we found something I have never seen before. The beach was not covered in shells but rocks. And when I say covered, I mean covered. These rocks were not just any rocks. The rocks either had holes in them, or a rust color was spiraling through the stone. I picked up one to keep. In my experience, when I've been inundated with something so different, God was getting my attention because He had a message for me.

The next morning, I was eager to go back to the beach to capture this unusual scene, and all the rocks were gone! I was puzzled! There were so many rocks on the beach the evening before. These rocks were not little. They had weight to them and about the average size of my hand.

I couldn't stop thinking about the rocks with holes, and then I remembered the story I was reading on the way there. The rock and the dishes had something in common, **brokenness**. And just like when the dishes are mended together with gold and become more valuable when we allow God to fill out brokenness with His golden goodness, the same occurs. The value of the experience is much more than we can imagine. That snowy beach trip was a blessing! Not only did He keep us safe, but I also came back refreshed and inspired. I definitely had to be brave and take a risk. And I am so glad I did!

Beautiful Burden

While this same year was filled with many blessings, it also was a year of great sadness. It is on February 12, 2018, that my beautiful, strong, loving Maw Maw went home to see her Lord. As the time approached, we didn't know how we would make it on the other side. She was ninety-seven, and she had always been there. We didn't want her to go, but she had to. However, it is like she made sure we would be ok.

For me, it came in the last visit with her. Once everyone left the room, I said, "Maw Maw, what are we going to do?" So, I picked up a magazine (one of her favorite past times) and started flipping through it. We talked about the birds and our love for honey. Then I came to a page with a caterpillar on it, and she said with such amazement and wonder, "Did you know a worm turns into a butterfly?" and

I said, "God is amazing, isn't He" and she agreed. That was our last visit, and even then, she was sowing seeds into me and speaking into my future. The lasting message to me was to get ready for a new birth. Life had felt especially hard over the last ten years, and at times I felt as low as a worm, but in her words, she was encouraging me that better days were ahead.

My Maw Maw was a wonderful woman. She was so strong, beautiful, and a blessing to all who knew her. She was simply amazing, and her legacy continues. I found a little Bible in her belongings in which she walks you through different scriptures, leading you to salvation (see A Message for Maw Maw). She embodied beauty! She loved fashion, sewing, and nature, especially birds and blooms. Her legacy that we must carry while beautiful is a strong charge to be poised and radiant in the face of difficult times, never letting go of the hand of our Father while leading our family by example. I am dedicated to carrying her legacy forward. In many ways, I feel her passing the baton was in her words, "do you know a worm turns into a butterfly." All the difficulty and challenge of becoming a butterfly is worth it upon viewing the beauty that that challenge reveals.

I am so blessed to have experienced and still experiencing strong, beautiful women that love the Lord in my life. From my courageous and supportive Mom to my uplifting sisters and cousin. I miss my Maw Maw greatly. I still feel close to her when I see the first signs of spring, smell the fragrance of blooms, enjoy the birds in the trees, feel the rain on my skin, and yes, see a beautiful flying butterfly.

A Message from Maw Maw

Alice Vienna Whittington Flowers (Maw Maw) left us these Scriptures in this order. The Scriptures were found in a Bible she received on September 29, 1971. She added notes in the margins and circled Scriptures instructing us to visit the following Scriptures in her little black New Testament Bible.

See page 313

Page 313 Circled in Red Reads–**Romans 3:23 (KJV)** For all have sinned, and come short of the glory of God

Turn to page 318

Page 318 Circled in Red Reads–**Romans 6:23 (KJV)** For the wages of sin is death, but the gift of God is eternal life through Jesus Christ our Lord.

Turn to page 388

Page 388 Circled in Red Reads–**Ephesians 2:8 (KJV)** For by grace are ye saved through faith; and that not of yourselves: it is the gift of God:

Now page 163

Page 163 Circled in Red Reads–**Luke 18:13 (KJV)** And the publican, standing afar off, would not lift up so much as his eyes unto heaven, but smote upon his breast, saying, God be merciful to me a sinner. (She writes, "Pray a Prayer Like this.")

Now page 189

Page 189 Circled in Red Reads–**John 3:16-17 (KJV)** For God so loved the world, that he gave his only begotten Son, that whosoever believeth in him should not perish, but have everlasting life. For God sent not his Son into the world to condemn the world; but that the world through him might be saved.

Now page 348

Page 348 Circled in Red Reads–**1 Corinthians 10:13 (KJV)** There hath no temptation taken you but such as is common to man: but God is faithful, who will not suffer you to be tempted above that ye are able; but will with the temptation also make a way to escape, that ye may be able to bear it.

Now page 321

Page 321 Circled in Red Reads—**Romans 8:38-39 (KJV)** For I am persuaded, that neither death, nor life, nor angels, nor principalities, nor powers, nor things present, nor things to come, Nor height, nor depth, nor any other creature, shall be able to separate us from the love of God, which is in Christ Jesus our Lord.

Now page 324

Page 324 Circled in Red Reads—**Romans 10:9-10 (KJV)** That if thou shalt confess with thy mouth the Lord Jesus, and shalt believe in thine heart that God hath raised him from the dead, thou shalt be saved. For with the heart, man believeth unto righteousness; and with the mouth, confession is made unto salvation.

Now page 367

Page 367 Circled in Red Reads—**2 Corinthians 6:2 (KJV)** For he saith, I have heard thee in a time accepted, and in the day of salvation have I succoured thee: behold, now is the accepted time; behold, now is the day of salvation.

Now page 257

Page 257 Circled in Red Reads–**Acts 8:35-39 (KJV)** Then Philip opened his mouth, and began at the same scripture, and preached unto him, Jesus. And as they went on their way, they came unto a certain water: and the eunuch said, See, here is water; what doth hinder me to be baptized? And Philip said, If thou believest with all thine heart, thou mayest. And he answered and said, I believe that Jesus Christ is the Son of God. And he commanded the chariot to stand still: and they went down both into the water, both Philip and the eunuch; and he baptized him. And when they were come up out of the water, the Spirit of the Lord caught away Philip, that the eunuch saw him no more: and he went on his way rejoicing.

Alice Vienna Whittington Flowers loved God and loved her family deeply.

September 16, 1920–February 12, 2018

I have no greater joy than to hear that my children are walking in the truth. 3 John 1:4 (NIV)

Scripture for the Journey: Purpose Bound

Verily, Verily I say unto you, except a grain of wheat falls unto the ground and dies, it abides alone; but if it dies, it brings forth much fruit. **John 12:24 (KJV)**

God's way is perfect. All the Lord's promises prove true. He is a shield for all who look to Him for protection. **Psalm 18:30 (NLT)**

Set your minds on things above, not on earthly things. **Colossians 3:2 (NIV)**

If you are willing and obedient, you shall eat the good of the land. **Isaiah 1:19 (ESV)**

I will instruct you and teach you in the way you should go; I will guide you with My eye. **Psalms 32:8 (NKJV)**

Trust in the Lord with all your heart and lean not on your own understanding; in all your ways acknowledge Him, and He will direct your paths. **Proverbs 3:5-6 (NKJV)**

For I know the plans I have for you, "declares the Lord, "plans to prosper you and not to harm you, plans to give you hope and a future. **Jeremiah 29:11(NIV)**

"Forget the former things; do not dwell on the past. See, I am doing a new thing! Now it springs up; do you not perceive it? I am making a way in the wilderness and streams in the wasteland. **Isaiah 43:18-19 (NIV)**

"Be strong and very courageous. Be careful to obey all the law my servant Moses gave you; do not turn from it to the right or to the left, that you may be successful wherever you go. Keep this Book of the Law always on your lips; meditate on it day and night, so that you may be careful to do everything written in it. Then you will be prosperous and successful. Have I not commanded you? Be strong and courageous. Do not be afraid; do not be discouraged, for the LORD your God will be with you wherever you go." **Joshua 1:7-9 (NIV)**

You did not choose me, but I chose you and appointed you so that you might go and bear fruit – fruit that will last – and so that whatever you ask in my name the Father will give you. **John 15:16 (NIV)**

Pebbles from the Path: Purpose Bound

Use this section to write notes from this chapter or jot down things that come to mind from your life in the area of purpose.

_____

_____

_____

_____

_____

_____

_____

_____

_____

Faith to Get Out of The Boat and Stay in the Water

*D*o you realize if faith is hope in something you can't see, it's impossible to please God without stepping into the unknown? Stepping into the unknown is exactly what I did when I decided to say yes to God's request to open The Retreat. Although God had prepared me for the journey, I feel like I was stripped down to 3oo like Gideon, maybe less, before I was given the go ahead sign.. And for some odd reason, I said ok and stepped into the water.

Now to be fair, as I mentioned before, God had prepared me for such a time as this. The part-time job at the Christian bookstore allowed me to see that finding a needle in a haystack was no problem for God. Soon I would begin to realize what He meant when He said, Ask for More! I wouldn't be hoping to get my resources in someone else's bookstore. He had plans for our own establishment, which was going to be much more than a bookstore.

I also learned through my journey that having access to Biblical truth and a supportive community helped me pull through some difficult times. The Biblical truth was found in the Word of God, excellent books, and ministers that enlightened me on a whole new level. My supportive community was my Mom, sisters, and cousin that poured into me regularly. We logged so many hours around the kitchen table. I can't even count the number of hours. My access to revelation knowledge and these experiences with my family made the difference, and I was inspired to replicate this experience for others through The Retreat.

Although it is taking some time to get there, this is how the journey began. By working at a Christian bookstore, I saw the need and benefit of a brick-and-mortar store. I knew that community was required to grow, heal, and transform. I then began feeling an overwhelming urge that I should be the one to open up a Christian bookstore, but in the natural, I wasn't in any position to start a business. I stepped out anyway. It is amazing how God sent word to me through customers that this is the way, walk in it. I will highlight a few here.

One young man was talking about how to know what the next step is and how to follow God's plans, and he said, "Do what's in front of you." This message, along with prayer, has helped me with many decisions. During a season of waiting for the Retreat, God sent a job to me and an opportunity to publish my book, so I did what was in front of me. This opened the door to a season of blessings.

During another encounter, a lady walked into the store, and for some reason, I was drawn to her. It isn't anything that I can even explain with words, but I went along with my normal greeting. When she arrived at the front to check out, we began to chat about The Retreat. She then pulled me aside and said God has been building your faith for this. He plans to provide for everything you need. She said, just ask for what you need, and He will provide. Another lady walks into the store, passing through from Florida, and wasn't finding what she came in the store to purchase. In the middle of our conversation, I had mention opening the bookstore. After our conversation, she walked out of the store and then shortly returned and began to proclaim that this was my Joshua Moment. She believed that relaying that message to me must have been the reason she had to stop by the store that day. Some naysayers tried hard to discourage me, but God would quickly come in with a Word that said keep moving forward.

It was sad to see the store close, but I was encouraged that God was doing a new thing. When looking at the timeline of events, God was working pretty fast, although it didn't always seem that way. Within one year of starting to work part-time, the store had plans to close, and I had plans for The Retreat. God began to open doors, and through donations, I gathered an abundance of store fixtures, office furniture, equipment, and inventory. It was amazing how God used the time I worked at the bookstore to grow me and speak to me. Although I thought the vision for The Retreat was birthed out of a need, I began to realize He had put the desire in my heart even before kids. I can't wait to see all that God is going to do.

I regularly get calls from people asking if The Retreat is open yet. My goal was to open The Retreat within one year of our local Christian store closing. However, this plan didn't know about a pandemic that was around the corner. With quarantine came questions, and I had to shift plans, but I am learning that is the nature of walking in faith and walking into your purpose. You have to be ok with not having all the answers and being uncomfortable at times. I am confident that what God started, He will finish. I just need to stay close to Him and trust this journey.

I have to admit sometimes, when I look around our space, and it is full of furniture and inventory for The Retreat, it feels like why did I do all of that to be right here. It feels like I have walked out into the water when I cast my eyes backward, I am too far to turn back now, but I am still far from the other side. However, I can't look at the waves. I must keep my eyes on God, and He will lead me exactly where He plans for me to be. I realize that the safest place to be, even if it's in the middle of a raging sea, is close to God.

Many times, God gives you the promise before your season of waiting. The promise keeps you during those long seasons of waiting. It reminds me of when God had downloaded all the themes, devotions, and activities for the Seeds that Last seed sacks. I thought that was what He was calling me to do. However, when it didn't work out as planned, and I had to pack away my Seeds that Last resources because there was no room or money for that dream in our current life, I was heartbroken. I was so sad. I had worked hard and didn't want this to be the end. Later, I heard Joanna Gaines describe a similar experience when she had to shut down her smaller store to focus on being a mom, but later God blessed her in more ways than she could ever imagine. God is not a respecter of persons. He has sent word and promised me great things. He has promised things that will not only bless my family but grow His Kingdom. Therefore, I am confident in this, I will see the goodness of the Lord in the land of the living. So, I will wait on the Lord; be strong and take heart and wait for the Lord (Psalm 27:13-14).

I continue to move toward The Retreat, I don't know the specifics of when this God-giving vision will be realized, but I continue to press. I look forward to doing ministry beside my family, providing Christian resources, community, and opportunities to collaborate with God's Church to expand His Kingdom. I look forward to making a difference in our community and beyond. So, as I await the fulfillment of the promises of God in my life, I encourage you to awaken all the dreams God has placed in your heart.

And be just like Peter who purposed in his heart, no matter what has happened this far, if God says so, you cast your net again. This Word speaks to all the times I have labored, only to come up short yet again. It encourages me that in His timing, the abundance and benefits will far outweigh all the failed attempts.

> When He had stopped speaking, He said to Simon, "Launch out into the deep and let down your nets for a catch." But Simon answered and said to Him, "Master, we have toiled all night and caught nothing; **nevertheless at Your word, I will let down the net**." And when they had done this, they caught a great number of fish, and their net was breaking. So, they signaled to *their* partners in the other boat to come and help them. And they came and filled both the boats so that they began to sink.
> **Luke 5:4-7 (NKJV)**

There is work to be done. God uses our surrender to the wilderness process to prepare us. Look at Jesus. It was no different in His walk.

> **And suddenly a voice *came* from heaven, saying, "This is My beloved Son, in whom I am well pleased. Then Jesus was led up by the Spirit**

into the wilderness to be tempted by the devil. Matthew 3:17 – 4:1 (NKJV)

My heart for helping others do life based on the Kingdom will be realized, and His promise to finish what He started and restore my years is coming to pass. When I look back, I could have rested more. It is like He planned it from the beginning, every turn, every reroute, every stoplight. **Although I thought that motherhood was sometimes keeping me from my purpose, God used it to perfectly bring me into my purpose**. He always keeps His promises, and He is faithful. I have to say I love My Lord repeatedly! He is so sweet and patient. What He starts, He finishes, so sit back and enjoy the ride!

Follow us on Instagram @theretreatllc, while we wait patiently on God's timing.

Scripture for the Journey: Water Walking Faith

Now faith is confidence in what we hope for
and assurance about what we do not see.
Hebrews 11:1 (NIV)

And without faith it is impossible to please
God, because anyone who comes to Him
must believe that He exists and that He
rewards those who earnestly seek Him.
Hebrews 11:6 (NIV)

So then faith comes by hearing and hearing
by the Word of God. **Romans 10:17 (NKJV)**

Ah, Sovereign Lord, you have made the
heavens and the earth by your great power
and outstretched arm. Nothing is too hard
for you. **Jeremiah 32:17 (NIV)**

I remain confident of this: I will see the
goodness of the Lord in the land of the
living. Wait for the LORD; be strong and
take heart and wait for the Lord. **Psalm
27:13-14 (NIV)**

That is what the Scriptures mean when
they say, "No eye has seen, no ear has
heard, and no mind has imagined what God

has prepared for those who love Him." **1 Corinthians 2:9 (NLT)**

He replied, "Because you have so little faith. Truly I tell you, if you have faith as small as a mustard seed, you can say to this mountain, 'Move from here to there,' and it will move. Nothing will be impossible for you." **Matthew 17:20 (NIV)**

Pebbles from the Path: Water Walking Faith

Use this section to write notes from this chapter or jot down things that come to mind from your life in the area of faith.

_____

_____

_____

_____

_____

_____

_____

_____

_____

_____

Nothing Missing
Nothing Broken

One day while taking an earlier morning walk, I noticed spider webs everywhere. The fog was thick and low. The grass was wet, and spider webs were everywhere I looked. They were in the trees, in the grass, on the fence just everywhere. At first, I was a little alarmed, thinking that there is a number of spiders out here. Then I thought to myself; God must be trying to show me something. I continued walking and chatting with Him. I was so happy to finally be taking the time to take care of myself and realizing the extra benefit of time spent with Him. It felt so good. And then He started unfolding the spider web.

If you have ever taken time to watch a spider make its web, it looks haphazard. It looks like the spider is just causally jumping through the air from one object to another with no real thought, no real plan. It's only when the spider is finished, and you step back that you see his masterpiece, a beautifully designed web that looks perfectly planned and carried out. I felt as if God was reminding me that, like the spider web, He has planned every aspect of my life. It may look and feel haphazard at times, but if I trust Him, in the end, it will be a beautifully designed masterpiece. I must be still and know that He is God, and He is planning every aspect of my life perfectly. I felt like I had a morning date with someone special with someone wise willing to share the secrets of life with me. I have learned through my journey that God speaks if you take the time to listen. He promises to guide us with His eyes and straighten our paths, but we must set aside time to abide.

You know, in the beginning, I mentioned I felt like something was missing. So, what was missing? I was a Christian and not a believer. I didn't fully understand who God was to me and who I was in Christ. When I surrendered to God and drew close to Him, my experiences made a believer out of me. Becoming a believer is about your experiences taking you to a deeper level in the Lord. These experiences change the way you do life. They are not superficial. And it is not about checking off practices to claim the title Christian. Becoming a believer through experiences transforms you inside out. Now I know from experience that He always keeps His promises. He never leaves you nor forsakes you. He is a Wonderful Provider, and He doesn't need your paycheck to provide. I now know He is a Healer, A Protector, A Way Maker, A Wonderful Counselor, A Comforter, A Friend, A Father, and so much more.

I also now know that I am a new creation. I am complete because I am in Him. Now there is no stopping me because I know whose I am and who I am in Christ. As long as I abide, as long as I stay close to Him, I can do all things through Christ, but without Him, nothing! My responses to life's circumstances can't be of the negative kind. I am learning to respond as the new woman I am. The new woman in Christ, for the old, has passed away, and the new has come. I am learning to think, see, talk, and do according to His Kingdom. And although it took some difficult circumstances, I am so glad that God loved me enough to strip that fake identity away and build up my new one. My purpose depended on it, and yours does too! **Surrender to God! Draw Close to Him! Your Purpose Depends On It!**

This Is My Story. Now it is time to Tell Your Story. Start Here.

And they overcame him by the blood of the Lamb, and by the word of their testimony; and they loved not their lives unto the death. Revelation 12:11 (KJV)

_____

_____

_____

_____

_____

_____

_____

_____

_____

_____

_____

_____

_____

_____

_____

_____

_____

_____

_____

_____

_____

_____

_____

_____

_____

_____

_____

_____

_____

_____

_____

_____

_____

_____

_____

_____

_____

_____

_____

_____

_____

_____

_____

_____

_____

_____

_____

_____

_____

_____

_____

_____

_____

_____

_____

_____

_____

_____

_____

_____

_____

_____

_____

Bibliography

Alan Dave Johnson, *Coffee Shop* (Production Co, 2014)

Bill Johnson, *Strengthen Yourself In the Lord: How to Release the Hidden Power of God In Your Life* (Destiny Image Publishers, Inc. 2015)

Dr. Caroline Leaf, *Who Switched Off My Brain?: Controlling Toxic Thoughts and Emotions* (Inprov, Ltd., 2009)

Graham Cooke YouTube Videos

Jackie Mize, *Supernatural Childbirth: Experiencing the Promises of God Concerning Conception and Delivery* (Harrison House Publishers, 1997)

Jeff Stilson, *Chris Rock's Good Hair* (HBO Films, LD Entertainment, & Chris Rock Productions, 2009)

Jennifer Kennedy Dean, *He Restores My Soul: A Forty-Day Journey Toward Personal Renewal* (Broadman & Holman Publishers, 1999)

Kelly J. Townsend, *Christ Centered Childbirth: Experiencing the Promises of God Concerning Conception and Delivery* (Four Winds Publications Illustrated edition, 2005)

Lisa Bevere, *Out of Control and Loving it!: Giving God Complete Control of Your Life* (Charisma House, 1996, 2006)

Neil T. Anderson, *Who I Am In Christ: A Devotional* (Bethany House Publishers, 2001)

Regina Franklin, *Who Calls you Beautiful* (Discovery House Publishers, 2004)

Dr. Rex Russell, *What the Bible Says About Healthy Living: Three Biblical Principles that will Change Your Diet and Improve Your Health* (Regal Books, 1996)

Stevie Smith, *Not Waving but Drowning* (1957)

Stormie Omartian, *The Power of a Praying Wife* (Harvest House Publishers, 1997)

Illustration Credits: Canva Pro

Please note that while these resources have benefited me and taught me many things, I do not endorse all the authors' views.

Resources

For more resources that help you heal, grow, and transform, visit Seeds that Last Website @ www.seedsthatlast.com – resources for children, moms, and women including the T.E.A. (Times of **T**ransformation **E**veryday **A**ll through the Day) Time Resources, the Home Manager, and information on essential oils

Your Purpose Depends On It! You will find all things book related @ **toshiajordan.com or yourpurposebook.com**

Stay informed about the progress **of The Retreat: More than a Bookstore @ www.theretreatllc.com**

Visit the Virtual Retreat. The Virtual Retreat allows you to take a break to reflect, reconnect, and reset. Here you will find inspiration based on the Word of God that will encourage you to do life better. A perfect place to gather while we wait on The Retreat. **Follow us on Instagram @ theretreatllc.**

Your Purpose Depends on You
Learning to Be Unapologetically Who God Created You to Be!

@toshiadjordan

CPSIA information can be obtained
at www.ICGtesting.com
Printed in the USA
BVHW070037130821
614283BV00001B/153

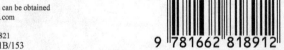